Lupe Velez
and Her Lovers

Lupe Velez
and Her Lovers

Floyd Conner

Barricade Books Inc.
New York

B
Velez

Published by Barricade Books, Inc.
61 Fourth Avenue
New York, NY 10003

Distributed by Publishers Group West
4065 Hollis
Emeryville, CA 94608

Copyright © 1993 by Floyd Conner

Printed in the United States of America.

Library of Congress Cataloging-in-Publication Data

Conner, Floyd, 1951 –
    Lupe Velez and her lovers / by Floyd Conner.
        p.   cm.
    ISBN 0-942637-96-8 : $20.00
    1. Velez, Lupe, 1906 – 1944. 2. Motion picture actors
and actresses — United States — Biography.   I. Title.
PN2287.V43C66   1993
791.43'028'092 — dc20
[B]   93-15899
                                                          CIP

0 9 8 7 6 5 4 3 2 1

Contents

Proem

The sometimes violent relationship with Lupe Velez was finally taking its toll on Gary Cooper. Lupe's attacks were becoming more frequent and Cooper feared for his life. He suffered a nervous breakdown. His doctor described his condition as a complete physical collapse. Cooper had lost forty pounds and suffered from jaundice. His doctors informed him that he would need at least a year of complete rest to fully recover. Cooper realized that the only way he would recover was to get away from Lupe.

Paramount agreed to grant him a six month leave of absence to recuperate. Cooper secretly planned an European vacation. He went incognito to the railroad station to catch the Twentieth Century to Chicago, unaware that he was being stalked. Lupe Velez had somehow learned of his departure, and decided that if she couldn't have him then no woman would.

Just as he was about to board the train, Lupe yelled, "Gary, you son-of-a-bitch!" She pulled out her revolver and fired. The bullet narrowly missed Cooper's head and he dove into the train. Lupe cursed her bad marksmanship as she hurried away before she could be apprehended.

1

The Mexican Hurricane

Maria Guadaloupe Velez de Villalobos, who would later squeeze the name to the less wieldy and more exotic Lupe Velez, was born in the tiny Mexican hamlet of San Luis de Potosi on July 18, 1908, the very day it was devastated by a hurricane. Gale force winds uprooted trees and tore roofs off the adobe houses. The violent weather was an appropriate introduction to the world for the woman who would become known as the "Mexican Hurricane."

Lupe's father Jacob was a colonel in dictator Porfirio Diaz's army, and during her childhood Mexico was torn by revolution and counter-revolution. Diaz, who ruled the country for thirty years, was overthrown when Lupe was just two. The pivotal figure in the Revolution was a bandit and cattle rustler named Pancho Villa, and it seemed that governments were being toppled daily. Somehow Jacob Villalobos, called "El Gallo" ("The Rooster") by his troops, always picked the losing side on which to fight, and young Maria acquired a taste for violence at an early age. As an adult she recalled riding with her father on military inspections and witnessing partisans being massacred by his troops.

Lupe's mother, Josefina, had been a diva with the Mexico City Opera, and once performed in a celebrated production of *La Boheme*. From Josefina, she got her expensive taste and love of jewelry. Years later, after becoming a movie star, Lupe showered Josefina with lavish gifts but they never seemed to be enough to satisfy her mother.

"I don't know what to do about her," Lupe told her friend, actress Esther Ralston.

"Why, you've given her diamonds, beautiful bracelets, fur coats, and the house," Ralston replied.

"She carried me for nine months and now she wants rent," Lupe explained.

Lupe had two sisters, Mercedes and Josefina, and a brother named Emigdio. By her own admission she was a hellion as a child, one with a vivid imagination and who spent much of her childhood in her own dream world. Her first ambition was to be a champion roller skater. At thirteen, Lupe was packed off to Our Lady of the Lake convent in San Antonio, Texas. It was hoped that the discipline of the convent would bring the rebellious teenager under control.

Lupe was an indifferent student. She later provided a capsule summary of her academic life: "Studied English. Liked to dance. Guess I wasn't much of a success as a student."

When she was fifteen, her father was killed in action during a battle in Mexico City and she was forced to quit school to help support her family. Her first job was as a salesgirl at the Nacionel Department Store where she earned four dollars a week. Lupe, the adolescent, loved to sing and dance and put aside money for dance lessons which cost thirty-seven cents per session.

In 1924, when she was sixteen, she was spotted by a Mexican producer named Alfeda who, impressed by her dancing ability and vibrant personality, offered her a featured role in his musical revue, *Ra-Ta-Plan*. Lupe was soon earning $350 per week (which was really big money in Mexico at the time) but quit when her demand for a $175 raise was rejected.

Lupe received offers to star in a Buenos Aires revue and to perform in Cuba, neither of which she accepted. The seventeen-year-old made ends meet by appearing in some film shorts in Mexico. Even as a teenager Lupe was already statuesque (her measurements were 37-26-35) and she briefly was a stripper in burlesque. Author Budd Schulberg, in his book *Moving Pictures*, suggested that Lupe supplemented her income in another manner. "Lupe herself made her theatrical debut in the raunchy burlesque houses of the city. Stagedoor Juanitos panted for her favors and Mama Velez would sell her for the evening to the highest bidder. Her price soared to thousands of pesos."

Her first big break occurred when Frank Woodward, a friend of the family, recommended Lupe to aging matinee idol Richard Bennett. For over thirty years Bennett had been one of the leading actors in American theater. At the time the Bennetts rivaled the Barrymores in popularity. His wife, Adrienne Morrison, was a well-known actress and their daughters, Barbara, Constance and Joan, would become film stars.

The dynamic Bennett, renowned for his deliberate, eloquent delivery, had just completed *They Knew What They Wanted* on Broadway in which he gave one of his most memorable performances as Tony, the aging grape grower. The year was 1925.

Bennett was searching for a fresh new face to play an ingenue role for a Los Angeles production of *The Dove*. Unable to find the right actress in California, Bennett went to Mexico to audition Lupe. He was so impressed that he telegrammed the play's producers, "Rush her to Hollywood!"

Teenager Lupe was elated about going to Hollywood, but was soon to learn that immigration officials had denied her entry into the United States because she was only seventeen.

"All the way back to Mexico City I cried," Lupe recalled. "But I'd show them. I would get to Hollywood some way. I appealed to our president, to the ministers, to everybody in Mexico City. After a lot of letter writing between Mexico City and Washington and what you call 'red tape' they said I could cross the border."

Misfortune awaited Lupe in California. No sooner had she gotten off the train in Los Angeles then she was robbed of all her money.

"By this time I was a week late and Mr. Bennett and the director kept asking, 'Where is that girl? Where is that damn girl?' Finally I got to the theater. The director took one look at me and yelled, 'Take that child off the stage, this is a rehearsal, not a kindergarten!' And I was supposed to play opposite Mr. Bennett! I tried my hardest to look older—I even wore padding but I only weighed ninety-two pounds."

The teenager's ingenue part given to a fifty-three-year-old actress named Dorothy Mackaye. Devastated at being fired, penniless and alone, Lupe accepted any work she could get. She agreed to appear at a benefit sponsored by the local traffic policemen. While performing in the show she caught the attention of Fanchon and Marco, the West Coast impresarios who signed her to appear as a featured dancer in their *Music Box Revue* which was scheduled to open shortly at Hollywood's Music Box Theater.

The star of the *Music Box Revue* was Fanny Brice, who had headlined nine *Ziegfeld Follies* and starred in numerous other revues. "I've done everything in the theater except marry the prop man," she quipped.

The *Music Box Revue* consisted of several of Fanny's favorite comic routines including her burlesques of Camille and Madame Pompadour. The highlight of the show was her song, "Make 'Em Laugh." Funloving and often outrageous, Fanny kept a pet rat which she fed ham and eggs. Her smiling, mischievous exterior masked a deeply troubled personal life. It was a difficult time emotionally for Brice. Her turbulent marriage to gangster Nicky Arnstein, which began in 1918, was coming to an end. Brice had always been attracted to scoundrels. She said, "I never liked the men I loved, and I never loved the men I liked."

She referred to Arnstein as "My Man." On the surface he was the perfect gentleman. Always impeccably dressed, Arnstein was a sophisticated middle-aged man with expensive taste in automobiles, furniture, and fine wines. He spent money freely, most of which had been earned by Fanny. With his dapper moustache, he looked more like a banker than a hoodlum. His close friend, W. C. Fields, based the flowery, over-blown language he used so brilliantly in countless films on Arnstein's speech.

Arnstein always seemed to have million dollar schemes which never panned out. He married Fanny in 1918 after serving two years in Sing Sing. In 1920, he was arrested as the mastermind of a scheme to steal $5 million in bonds from Wall Street. Fanny spent six years and most of her savings trying to defend him from the charges but eventually he was convicted and served two years in Leavenworth. In September 1927, a few months after the Hollywood *Music Box Revue* closed, Brice filed for divorce, citing Arnstein's flagrant infidelity.

The show had opened on February 2, 1927, to disappointing reviews. *Variety* described it as "a vaudeville show lacking in brilliance and novelty." Audiences were familiar with most of Brice's routines from previous tours. The *Music Box Revue* closed on April 7 after a modest nine-week run.

Although the show had not been a success, the fledgling Lupe had impressed Fanny Brice with her dancing ability and effervescent personality. Brice contacted Florenz Ziegfeld in New York and recommended Lupe for one of his Broadway extravaganzas. As a result, Lupe, in 1927, was offered a sixteen-week contract to perform in Ziegfeld's *Rio Rita*, but she never made it to New York. Suddenly Lupe Velez was a hot property. At the same time, Harry Rapf of MGM approached Lupe about doing a screen test. He was surprised when she initially turned him down.

"I am going to New York to get me a good job in the *Follies*," she explained. "Anyhow, I am not pretty like movie girls."

Rapf persisted and Lupe reluctantly agreed to the screen test, which consisted of her walking briskly before the camera. Producer Hal Roach of the Pathé Studio saw the test and signed her to a contract. Roach realized that nubile Lupe's shapely figure was ideal for his "bathing beauty" comedies. Many actresses had already used the "bathing beauty" route to stardom. When Lupe joined Pathé, future stars Carole Lombard and Jean Harlow were on the payroll.

In August 1927, Lupe Velez made her American film debut as an extra in a Charley Chase comedy short, *What Women Did for Me*. Roach was pleased with what he saw and the next month he gave Lupe a larger part in a two-reeler, *Sailors Beware!*, featuring the newly-formed comedy team of Stan Laurel and Oliver Hardy.

Laurel and Hardy would become one of the most successful comedy teams of all time. They made 105 films together including classic comedies such as *The Music Box*. Almost every film featured Stan Laurel as a dim-witted, whimpering sap and Oliver Hardy as the slow-burning victim of his misadventures. Actually they made more films separately than as a team. Laurel appeared in 76 films without Hardy and Ollie appeared in 213 films without Stan.

Stan Laurel had been a comedian for more than twenty years before he was teamed with Oliver Hardy. Born in Ulverston, Lancashire, England in 1890, Laurel was an understudy for Charlie Chaplin when the two young comedians came to America in 1910 as

members of the Fred Karno Company. For a number
of years Laurel (then known as Stanley Jefferson)
toured the vaudeville circuit as a Chaplin imitator. He
began appearing in films in around 1917.

Oliver Hardy's background was quite different from
that of his future partner. He was born into a distinguished Georgia family in 1892, and broke into show
business at eighteen as the operator of a movie theater.
Once he turned to acting, he was usually cast as a
villain.

The teaming of Laurel and Hardy happened almost
by accident. Laurel signed with the Roach studio as a
director. In 1926, he was directing a short, *Get 'Em
Young*, in which Oliver Hardy had a small part as a
butler. The two had appeared together briefly (although not as a team) in a film, *Lucky Dog*, nine years
previously. In that one, Hardy played a robber who
held up Laurel.

One day, during the filming of *Get 'Em Young*, the
rotund Hardy, who was a gourmet cook, burned himself preparing a leg of lamb. Reed-thin Laurel was
forced to act in the movie until Hardy recovered.
When the latter returned, it was apparent to producer
Hal Roach that there was a special chemistry between
the two players. Leo McCarey, who later directed classic comedies such as *Duck Soup* and *The Awful Truth*,
suggested the teaming of Stan Laurel and Oliver
Hardy. Laurel, who preferred directing to acting, initially opposed the idea.

In *Sailors Beware!*, Stan plays a dim-witted cabbie
who drives a notorious jewel thief (Anita Garvin) to the
docks. Accompanied by her midget husband (Tiny San-
ford) who is disguised as a baby, she boards a luxury

liner in the hopes of robbing the rich passengers. By mistake, Stan and his cab are loaded aboard as cargo. Considered a stowaway, Stan is put to work by Ollie, the ship's purser.

Lupe Velez plays the haughty Baroness Behr, one of the passengers. She appears in a slapstick poolside scene which culminates with Stan shoving Lupe into the water. Stan becomes an unlikely hero when he foils the thieves' plan by exposing the baby's true identity. The film has a bizarre ending in which the enraged midget beats up Ollie.

Already Lupe's outrageous antics on the set were being noticed. Costar Anita Garvin remembered, "Crazy Lupe! She was a little wild Mexican—with her little chihuahua. They'd get the chihuahua and hide the poor thing in the cameraman's sack that was on the tripod. And she'd go storming all over the place demanding "Where's my baby, my chihuahua?'"

Garvin also recalled Lupe being self-conscious about her diminutive size. "She was tiny [barely five-feet tall]. She'd say 'Anita! You are so nice and fat and I am so skinny.'"

Once Lupe started acting in films she was no longer interested in Broadway. And she was no longer satisfied with being a "bathing beauty" or an extra in comedy shorts. Lupe wanted to be a movie star. She did not have long to wait, after leaving the Roach lot.

2

The Gaucho

One day in 1927 Lupe was spotted in the courtyard of the Egyptian Theater by talent scout Ted Reed, who at the time worked for Douglas Fairbanks, then the biggest star in Hollywood. Fairbanks was looking for a young actress to play the Wild Mountain Girl in his next film, *The Gaucho*. Once he saw Lupe, Fairbanks agreed that she was perfect for the part and his studio, United Artists, signed the nineteen-year-old Lupe to a five-year contract.

The studio began a publicity campaign to promote its newest property. In those days it was common for an actor's background to be fabricated to make him or her appear more glamorous. Lupe decided to take the opposite approach. She claimed that her mother had been a prostitute and that she herself had come to Hollywood when she was only fourteen. Later, when the studio took credit for making her a star, Lupe objected in her broken English.

"Pooh, I am always a star! When I came from Mexico I am not yet sixteen. I have not a peso, but even before Douglas Fairbanks put me in *The Gaucho* I know I am a star already."

Douglas Fairbanks and wife Mary Pickford were considered the closest thing to royalty in Hollywood. Fairbanks was known as the "King of the Swashbucklers" and was the movies' first great action hero. His daring acrobatics were featured in such silent classics as *The Mark of Zorro, Robin Hood, The Three Musketeers,* and his masterpiece, *The Thief of Bagdad.* In his memoirs, Charlie Chaplin explained Fairbanks' appeal, "He had extraordinary magnetism and charm and a genuine boyish enthusiasm which he conveyed to the public."

Dashingly handsome Douglas Fairbanks seemed possessed with supercharged energy, both on and off screen. At parties he would leap over furniture and do handstands on tables. Occasionally, he would dive under the dinner table and grab the ankles of the female guests.

His wife, Mary Pickford, was the cinema's first superstar. Almost singlehandedly, she created the star system in Hollywood. She was born Gladys Smith in Toronto in 1893. In 1909, D. W. Griffith, insisting that she was too fat to be in movies, offered her $5-a-day to sign with Biograph. Pickford demonstrated her shrewd business savvy by insisting on $10. She became known to fans as "America's Sweetheart" and "The Girl With The Curls." By 1916 her weekly salary had increased from $50 to $10,000.

In 1919, Douglas Fairbanks, Mary Pickford (the screen's first great female star) Charlie Chaplin, and director D. W. Griffith formed their own studio, United Artists. The next year Fairbanks and Pickford were married. As a wedding present, Fairbanks gave Pickford a converted hunting lodge, a magnificent L-shaped Tudor residence that would be named Pickfair. It was located atop Summit Drive, at the pinnacle of Beverly Hills. From their gardens, Fairbanks and Pickford could look down upon their domain.

The couple became the official host and hostess of Hollywood. Celebrities and royalty, an international who's who, visited Pickfair—Albert Einstein, Henry Ford, Babe Ruth, Charles Lindbergh, Amelia Earhart, the Duke of York (the future King George VI of England), and virtually every star in Hollywood. Guests were served on a gold dinner service which had once been a present from Napoleon to Josephine.

The Gaucho (shot in black and white with Technicolor sequences) marked the first time Fairbanks and Pickford had appeared in the same film. Fairbanks was cast in the title role while Pickford made a cameo appearance as the madonna-like Our Lady of the Shrine. The Gaucho, sort of an Argentine version of Robin Hood, makes his living as a bandit. His lover is a gypsy girl portrayed by Lupe Velez. The film opens on a small village where a young girl, having fallen from a mountain ledge, is saved from certain death by an apparition of the Madonna (Pickford). The vision is declared a miracle and the village becomes a shrine. "The City of the Miracle" becomes rich with the gold offerings of pilgrims.

Lured by the wealth, The Gaucho (Fairbanks) seizes the city and robs the shrine of its gold. He attempts to seduce the "Girl of the Shrine," but his gypsy lover angered by his attempted infidelity, stabs him. To make matters worse, a leper infects him with the dreaded disease. Just as the Gaucho is about to commit suicide, the girl he had tried to seduce (Eve Southern) leads him to the healing waters of the shrine. He sees the vision of the Madonna and is miraculously cured. The Gaucho promises to reform, but is imprisoned when his lover betrays him to the authorities. The Gaucho escapes, and in a somewhat unbelievable ending, reunites with his mountain girl lover.

Lupe Velez brought a new kind of sex appeal to film. Previously, foreign actresses such as Vilma Banky and Pola Negri, as well as Lupe's Mexican compadre, Dolores Del Rio, had been exotic beauties. Lupe brought an earthiness to her roles which was new to the movies. Her love scenes with Douglas Fairbanks caused a sensation. The two lovers attacked each other on screen in an almost combative fashion. One critic described their lovemaking as "a pugilistic encounter."

The scene in which they first meet in a tavern demonstrates their animal attraction. Fairbanks lassoes Lupe and draws her close to him. He kisses her firmly on the lips then blows smoke into her face. Lupe responds by beating him with her fists.

One of the reasons Lupe had gotten the part was due of her combative nature. When Fairbanks first saw Lupe she was standing with a chihuahua under her arm. His initial impression was that she was too placid for the role. A member of the crew stole Lupe's dog as a joke. When she discovered what had happened she beat the man mercilessly. Fairbanks signed her on the spot.

"He found out I am not placid also, later on, too, when he told me to take my shoes off. I will not do that, I have feet like a peacock bird."

Lupe claimed that she had her first date with F. Richard Jones, the film's director. "When I was working in *The Gaucho* they all made fun of my age. 'Why are you not in school, baby?' they ask. 'Where are your pigtails?' they say. Well, I show them. I have the very first date of my life with the director of the movie. I loved him desperately, even if he did pat me on my head like a little girl on the movie lot.

"I spent all of my money on two white fox furs and I started out on my first date with the man I love — to the movie around the corner. He delivered me home at ten and wanted to know why I was crying when he left me — with a pat on my head!"

The love scenes between Lupe Velez and Douglas Fairbanks were not confined to the set. They both possessed an extraordinary zest for life. Throughout her life Lupe was attracted to athletic men and Fairbanks, despite being in his mid-forties, had maintained his magnificent physique. Mary Pickford was extremely jealous and always stood just outside of camera range to insure that Fairbanks' love scenes did not become too realistic. Despite her precautions, cracks were beginning to form in what everyone considered to be Hollywood's perfect marriage.

Because her part was small in *The Gaucho,* Pickford was able to work on another film, *My Best Girl,* at the same time. Although she was thirty-four, she was still typecast as a girl half her age. Her costar was a handsome young actor named Buddy Rogers who immediately fell in love with her. "I think he's got a crush on me," Pickford told her mother. Her mother shocked Mary by encouraging the romance. She was angry with Fairbanks because he had repeatedly snubbed her at Pickfair. She was determined to do whatever she could to undermine the marriage.

One day Fairbanks appeared unexpectedly on the set of *My Best Girl*. Pickford and Rogers were right in the midst of a steamy love scene. After they kissed, Fairbanks hurried from the set. "It was more than jealousy," he admitted. "I suddenly felt afraid."

His insecurity drove him right into Lupe's arms. Their relationship, like many of Lupe's, was brief and intense but it had a lasting impact on Fairbanks' marriage. Lupe Velez was the only one of Fairbanks' co-stars to make Pickford jealous. She resented her husband's desire to be with Lupe. For the first time Pickford began to have doubts about herself. She felt insufficient and wondered if she was still attractive to her husband. According to her close friends, she brooded about the affair for years.

The Gaucho had its premier at Grauman's Casino Theater in Hollywood on November 24, 1927. Audiences were charged $1.50 per person, six times the normal ticket price. The film received mixed reviews. The striking photography and the spectacular action sequences were praised as was the experimental use of a new process called Technicolor. However, most critics agreed that the best thing about the movie was the sexy newcomer, Lupe Velez. The film was released nationwide in early 1928 and Morduant Hall, film critic of *The New York Times*, wrote:

"Miss Velez gives a capital characterization as the Mountain Girl. Whether in rags or lace, she gives blow-for-blow to the men who get in her way."

Variety agreed: "[Velez] scores 100 percent and is established as a feminine Fairbanks. She is a beauty and has that freshness that goes with youth. When it comes to acting she does not have to step aside for anyone. They put on a rave about Dolores Del Rio for more than two years out here. Now it's going to go for Lupe. This kid has a great sense of comedy value to go with her athletic prowess."

Lupe reacted to her sudden fame, "Was I happy when *The Gaucho* opened and the public was nice to Lupe? Not happy — delirious!"

While *The Gaucho* marked the real beginning of Lupe's movie career, in many ways it was the beginning of the end for Douglas Fairbanks and Mary Pickford. For the first time critics were making note of Fairbanks' age (forty-four). *The Jazz Singer*, Hollywood's first talking picture, had just been released and Fairbanks, like many other stars, had doubts about his future in talkies.

Mary Pickford faced an even greater crisis. At thirty-four, she was too old to continue to play little girls. "I am sick of playing Cinderella," she said. She took two years off after *The Gaucho* to reassess her career. Pickford did the unthinkable by cutting off her famous golden curls. Her fans were outraged. "You would have thought I had murdered someone." Her comeback role as a flapper in *Coquette* signaled an end to innocence. Hollywood rewarded her courage by giving her an Academy Award for Best Actress but, in reality, her career was over. Pickford retired from the screen a few years later in 1933.

The storybook marriage was also coming to an end. Pickford withdrew to the security of Pickfair. She had her personal horoscope delivered to her each morning at breakfast and planned her day accordingly. When Douglas Fairbanks, Jr. married Joan Crawford, Pickford warned Mommie Dearest not to have any children. Still obsessed with being "America's Sweetheart," she could not face becoming a grandmother. Pickford began to drink heavily, usually doing it in her bathroom to conceal it from her guests. Her hopes for a new career on radio, interviewing the stars, were dashed when Louella Parsons, who already had her own program, sabotaged the project by threatening stars who appeared on Pickford's broadcasts.

Douglas Fairbanks' career was also on the decline. A series of flops demonstrated that he had lost his box-office appeal. He went to England hoping to revitalize his career. Fairbanks made his last film, *The Private Life of Don Juan,* in 1934. He fell in love with an Englishwoman, Lady Sylvia Ashley. Mary Pickford filed for divorce in 1935 and Fairbanks married Ashley the following year. In 1937, Pickford wed the much younger Buddy Rogers, the actor she had kissed in *My Best Girl* a decade earlier, and their marriage survived until her death in 1979. Douglas Fairbanks died of a heart attack in 1939.

Mary Pickford invested her money wisely and amassed a fortune of over $50 million. As the years passed her drinking increased. She consumed up to a quart of whiskey a day. The woman who was once the

premier hostess in Hollywood became a recluse, roam-
ing the halls of Pickfair on many a sleepless night.
Although she was unable to rest she spent much of the
day in bed. "I've been working since I was five and I
deserve the rest," she said.

3

Mix, Kennedy, Gable, and The Little Tramp

Lupe Velez had become a star overnight. At nineteen, she was already considered the hottest sex symbol in Hollywood. Tabloids referred to her as the "Mexican Wildcat" or the "Hot Tamale." Still starstruck, she was constantly in the company of leading men.

One of the actors with whom she was seen in public was Tom Mix. At the time he was the top cowboy star in pictures. Mix was the first to bring showmanship to the Western. The flamboyant Mix wore frilly white cowboy suits. His horsehair belt had a diamond studded buckle with the inscription: "Tom Mix, America's Champion Cowboy." He dubbed his horse "Tony the Magnificent."

His gift for exaggeration rivaled that of Baron Munchausen. According to Mix, he was born in a log cabin in El Paso, Texas. When he was seven years old he claimed he earned his living as a knife thrower in a circus. While still a teenager he became a soldier of fortune. During the Spanish American War Mix claimed he was one of Teddy Roosevelt's Rough Riders and was wounded in the face leading the charge up San Juan Hill. After he recuperated, he travelled to the Philippines where he participated in the Siege of Manila. He fought on both sides of the Boer War, breaking horses for the British. Next, he claimed to have fought courageously in the Boxer Rebellion, suffering a superficial wound on the forehead. All told, Mix claimed to have suffered 21 separate knife and bullet wounds. Later, when he became a star, he marketed a fold-out chart which showed the location of the wounds and how they were inflicted.

Mix, weary of war, traveled west where he became a Texas Ranger, bounty hunter, and a United States marshal. When the Mexican Revolution broke out he went south of the border to fight. Mix was captured by the rebels and was just about to be shot by a firing squad when he miraculously escaped. Amazingly, everyone believed these tall tales for years.

Tom Mix was actually born in Pennsylvania and later joined the army, seeing only routine battery duty during the Spanish American War and never leaving the United States. In 1902, at the urging of his wife, he deserted. In constant fear of being apprehended, he went west to avoid capture.

Mix drifted from job to job, joining a Wild West show in 1905 and mastering cowboy skills such as riding, roping, and shooting. Five years later, producer William Selig was in the area making a documentary entitled *Ranch Life in the Great Southwest*. The purpose of the film was to show how cattle were raised and marketed. Selig thought that Mix's ranch provided an ideal location. Mix was put in charge of taking care of the livestock. He pestered the director to appear in the movie and was given a small role as a bronco buster.

Mix moved to Hollywood where he used his cowboy skills to land a job as a stuntman. Soon he got his first starring role in *The Range Rider*. While his fantasies of being a war hero were false he was no fake on the set. Mix did most of his stunts and his horsemanship was the best in Hollywood. His star rose quickly and in the 1920s he was the highest paid actor in Hollywood, earning $17,500 a week. By comparison, a young Gary Cooper was making $50 a week at the time.

Director D. W. Griffith could not understand Mix's appeal. "He can't act, but he can ride like hell and everybody loves him. I don't know why." Griffith did admit, "Tom Mix can burn a hole through a camera by merely staring at it."

Mix was instrumental in the discovery of another movie legend, John Wayne. Mix was a fan of the powerhouse University of Southern California football team known as the Thundering Herd. One of the star players was a hulking end from Iowa named Marion Morrison. The son of a druggist, Morrison was nicknamed the "Duke" after a pet airedale terrier he had as a child.

Mix became friends with Morrison and got him a $35 a week summer job at Fox in exchange for season tickets to the football games. Morrison's job was in the prop department and his first assignment was to tend a flock of geese. The pay was so poor that he was forced to live in a garage. When Mix saw the young Morrison at the studio he didn't even acknowledge his presence, a snub the Duke never forgot.

Morrison was working as an assistant property man

on a film being directed by John Ford. Ford often made him the butt of cruel practical jokes but the Duke quietly accepted being the director's whipping boy and earned his respect. During the filming of *Men Without Women* he agreed to attempt a dangerous underwater stunt which experienced stuntmen had refused to perform. As a result he was rewarded with a bit part in the movie.

Morrison was a prop man for three years before his big break occurred. According to legend he was unloading a truckload of furniture when he was noticed by director Raoul Walsh. Walsh was intrigued by his distinctive lumbering gait and arranged for a screen test. Morrison was signed to a $75 a week contract and cast in Walsh's next film, *The Big Trail*. Walsh didn't like Morrison's name and decided to change it. He was a Revolutionary War buff and named him after his favorite general, "Mad Anthony" Wayne. Walsh thought that Marion sounded too much like a woman's name and changed it to John. John Wayne went on to make 153 films and became the greatest western star in movie history.

When Mix met Lupe Velez, he had already been through several marriages. His attitude toward women was less than chivalrous. He threatened his fourth wife by twirling a loaded gun on his finger.

"When a man's been married half-a-dozen times any sentiment about anniversaries is as cold as the ashes of last year's campfire. Paying all them alimonies sort of drains out the romance."

Although he was in his late forties, Mix was a handsome, vibrant man with the muscular physique of a man half his age. He was tall, lanky, with a prominent nose and a strong jaw. Mix dyed his hair black — almost blue. He told Gene Autry, "The Lord has been good to me. He preserved my hair. I can sure keep it black for Him."

Mix was a deliberate talker, partly because he had constant trouble with his false teeth. He claimed that he had lost his teeth when he had been shot in the face during the Spanish American War. Every few sentences he'd have to reach up with his thumb and click his teeth in place.

Lupe Velez believed a movie star should live like one and no one had more star trappings than Tom Mix. He resided in a Spanish style Hollywood mansion equipped with nine marble bathrooms. The floors of his home were covered with animal skin rugs and trophies of big game hunts hung on the walls. His TM brand was stamped on nearly everything he owned. Outside the estate an electric sign flashed his initials. Mix's seven car garage was filled with classics. His favorite was a custom-built car with a saddle and steer horns on the hood.

Both Lupe and Tom shared a love of boxing. Mix had a regulation boxing ring installed in his dressing room to help him keep fit. By nature Mix was easygoing but he also had a violent side. One night he and Lupe were having a tete-à-tete in a nightclub when they were interrupted by Vince Barnett, a character actor who had the reputation of being Hollywood's biggest practical joker. When Barnett tried to engage in conversation with Lupe, Mix jumped up and began to choke him.

As Mix's popularity began to wane so did Lupe's interest in him. His contract was not renewed by Fox and his movie career might have been over were it not for the intervention of Joseph Kennedy. Oddly, Tom Mix was instrumental in the making of the Kennedy fortune.

Joseph Kennedy, the Boston financier and family patriarch, had made a small fortune in the 1920s by manipulating stocks when the market was unregulated. During Prohibition he became a high-class bootlegger, importing Irish whiskeys and French champagnes into the United States. When he came to Hollywood he hoped to make another quick killing.

Kennedy assumed control of Film Booking Office, a second-rate studio churning out B movies. Needing a big star to give his FBO credibility, he signed Tom Mix at a salary of $15,000 per week. Kennedy stayed in Hollywood long enough to be involved in a notorious affair with actress Gloria Swanson. By the time he returned to Massachusetts, Kennedy had merged his holdings to form a major studio, RKO, and walked away with a $5 million profit.

Joseph Kennedy got out of the stock market before it crashed in 1929 but Tom Mix wasn't so lucky. He lost more than a million dollars when the bottom fell out and was forced to sell his Beverly Hills mansion and Arizona ranch. Charged with income tax evasion, he was forced to pay $150,000 in arrears.

Mix's love of fast cars ended on an Arizona highway in 1940. A flash flood had washed out a bridge and Mix, driving his white Cord convertible at a high rate of speed, failed to negotiate a turn. Tom Mix, America's favorite cowboy, died instantly from a broken neck. To honor him, a statue of a riderless horse was erected on the side of the road.

Lupe, after dumping Mix, had already caught the eye of Clark Gable. Born in Cadiz, Ohio, in 1901, Gable had been a muleskinner, timekeeper in a rubber factory, and a lumberjack before turning to acting. He travelled west, riding the rails as a hobo. Gable was working as a telephone repairman in Oregon when he was called to fix the phone of Josephine Dillon. She operated her own drama school and recommended that the tall, rugged Gable should study acting.

Dillon accompanied Gable to Hollywood where they were married in 1924. Gable made an inauspicious stage debut when he tripped and fell on his face making his first entrance. He made several unsuccessful screen tests. Irving Thalberg, boy wonder at MGM took one look at the test and exclaimed, "Good God! No, not that! Take it away." Jack Warner asked his assistant, "Why did you throw away five hundred dollars of our money on a test on that big ape?" Producer Howard Hughes was appalled by Gable's big ears and remarked, "He looks like a taxicab with both doors open."

Gable was so discouraged that he was about to leave Hollywood when MGM unexpectedly signed him to a one year contract. At the time he in no way resembled the handsome actor who would become known as the "King." His teeth were crooked and rotten and he had not yet grown his trademark moustache. The dentist did a bad job capping his teeth and it was necessary for him to get dentures. His false teeth was the most closely guarded secret on the lot, but Gable was never self-conscious about them. In fact, at parties he would remove them to do tricks with them.

When he met Lupe, Gable had already been married

twice, both times to older women. "I'll take the older woman every time," he said. In spite of this preference, Gable had countless affairs with women of all ages. Once he was shown a publicity photograph which featured all the major MGM actresses. He admired the photo for a moment and boasted, "What a wonderful display of beautiful women, and I've had all of them." Actress Joan Blondell expressed his universal appeal to women when she said, "Gable affected all females, unless they were dead."

Despite his enormous sexual appetite, Gable had the reputation of being a lousy lover. He was aware that Lupe had the habit of making public the sexual prowess of her lovers. Gable's fear of embarrassing revelations caused him to break off his relationship with Lupe. He told a friend, "She'll be all over town telling everyone what a lousy lay I am."

Lupe's romantic liaisons in 1928 with Charlie Chaplin (who liked his women young) was one of tinseltown's best-kept secrets. Writer Adela Rogers St. Johns called the relationship, "one of the most secretive yet most torrid romances in the history of Hollywood."

Charlie Chaplin was born in England in 1888. His father was an alcoholic who deserted the family shortly after Charlie was born and his mentally unstable mother was frequently institutionalized. Chaplin spent most of his childhood in orphanages and poorhouses. At the age of eight Chaplin went to work, earning 60 cents a week as a janitor. As a youth he worked various jobs including being a glassblower, clog dancer, and a lather boy in a barbershop.

Chaplin toured America with a music hall troupe for several years before settling in Hollywood in 1914.

Mack Sennett recognized his potential and signed him to star in a series of comic shorts. One day in the wardrobe room Chaplin put on a pair of Fatty Arbuckle's pants, Ford Sterling's oversized shoes, Mack Swain's fake moustache, and a bowler hat borrowed from his father-in-law. The "Little Tramp" character was born. Within two years Chaplin was earning $10,000 a week and was the most popular comedian in films.

Chaplin made some of the most brilliant comedies in film history but his scandalous private life threatened his career. Unlike Gable, Chaplin preferred teenage girls in his sexual encounters. His first wife, Mildred Harris, was 16 years old when he married her because she told him she was pregnant. The pregnancy proved to be false but when the couple did have a child it turned out to be hideously deformed and died shortly after birth. Chaplin and Harris divorced in 1920.

Chaplin first saw his next wife, Lilita Grey, when she was six years old. The daughter of a waitress working at Kitty's Come-On-In, Lilita was a beautiful child with a gay manner who left a lasting impression on Chaplin. His obsession with the young Lilita was the inspiration for Vladimir Nabokov's controversial bestselling novel, *Lolita*. He signed her to a movie contract when she was 12 years old and she made her film debut in *The Kid*. At the signing, the young Lilita was heard to say, "Goody. Goody."

In 1923, Chaplin began filming his masterpiece, *The Gold Rush*. He shocked Hollywood when he announced that the 14-year-old Lilita would play the female lead. Chaplin commented to a friend that he thought Lilita was the most beautiful girl he had ever seen. Now that he had got her into films his next step was to get her into bed.

During shooting he could no longer restrain his passion. Chaplin tried to molest Lilita in his hotel room, finally consummating their love on the bathroom floor. According to Lilita he told her, "I could have had a thousand women but I want to be naughty with you."

Lilita was 16-years-old when she became pregnant. Chaplin reluctantly replaced her in *The Gold Rush* with Georgia Hale. Fearing a scandal that could ruin his career, he asked Lilita to have an abortion. When she refused he offered her $20,000 to marry another man. Desperate, he even suggested that she commit suicide by throwing herself off a train. On November 24, 1924, Chaplin married Lilita Grey.

The shotgun marriage proved to be a living hell for Chaplin. His mother-in-law virtually took over his mansion, throwing lavish parties at Chaplin's expense. To get away Chaplin took long drives at night and often slept at the athletic club. Although he was a millionaire, Chaplin was notorious for his penny-pinching ways. His home, which was built by his set department to save money, was known as "Breakaway House" because it was constantly falling apart. He spent almost nothing on his wife's wardrobe declaring that "Two dresses a year were enough for any woman."

The marriage was doomed from the start and when the couple divorced in 1927, the trial was one of the most sensational in Hollywood history. Lilita accused Chaplin of blatant adultery with at least five different women and engaging in degenerate sexual acts. Much of Chaplin's private sexual life was made public. Lilita testified that Chaplin, always the showman, asked her to have sex in front of an audience. As part of foreplay, he recited erotic passages from D. H. Lawrence's novel, *Lady Chatterly's Lover.*

The public's reaction to the trial was overwhelming. Thousands of transcripts of the trial were sold. For a time Chaplin's films were banned in some countries. Chaplin had a nervous breakdown and his hair turned white overnight.

"What I've gone through has aged me ten years," he admitted.

Lilita Grey was awarded a settlement of nearly a million dollars and Chaplin was forced to pay an even larger sum in legal fees. Newspaper headlines called the settlement "The Second Gold Rush." To make matters worse, the Internal Revenue Service told Charlie he owed $1,133,000 in back taxes. Personal tragedy struck when his mother suddenly died of a stroke. Chaplin became deeply depressed and many of his friends worried that he might commit suicide.

It was at this time that Lupe Velez entered his life. Besides his personal problems, he was feeling doubts about his future in the movies. Sound films were being developed and Chaplin vehemently opposed them. He bet William Randolph Hearst $100 that talkies were a passing fad that wouldn't last a year. "Motion pictures need sound as much as Beethoven's symphonies need lyrics," he proclaimed. When sound pictures replaced silents, Chaplin was the last to make the conversion. He did not make his first all-talking picture, The Great Dictator, until 1940.

Chaplin, the master comedian, had a secret desire to

become a serious actor. When the studio proposed filming the life of Christ, Chaplin volunteered to play Jesus.

"I'm the logical choice," he argued. "I look the part, I'm a Jew, and I'm a comedian. And I'm an atheist so I'd be able to look at the character objectively." When the studio bosses rejected his blasphemous suggestion Chaplin exclaimed, "There is no God! If there is one I dare Him to strike me dead."

Few in the film community knew of the Velez-Chaplin affair. They made one of their few public appearances together at the premiere of Colleen Moore's film, *Lilac Time*. At forty, Chaplin was twice Lupe's age but he was still a vigorous lover. Although he was small in height, his penis was so large that it was referred to as "the eighth wonder of the world." Lupe was one of his few lovers who could match his prowess in bed.

Lupe's carefree manner did much to restore Chaplin's spirit. His film, *The Circus*, was a critical and box office success and earned him an Academy Award nomination. He no longer needed Lupe to rebuild his confidence. Lupe was only twenty but she was already too old for his taste for little girls. Chaplin preferred young women he could dominate, and no one was about to dominate Lupe Velez. With the shotgun wedding to Lilita Grey in his recent past he was in no hurry to make another trip to the altar. Lupe was also in no rush to get married. She wanted to establish her film career before becoming involved in a lasting relationship.

4

The Lady of the Pavements

Lupe's follow-up film to *The Gaucho* was called *Stand and Deliver* (1928). Her costar was a handsome Rudolph Valentino lookalike named Rod La Rocque. Warner Oland, who would later gain fame playing detective Charlie Chan, was cast in a supporting role as Chika, the bandit. (Despite being of Swedish descent, Oland was typecast in Oriental roles). Donald Crisp served as producer and director for the film, as well as acting in it. Crisp, a native of Scotland, would appear in over 400 films and would be honored with an Oscar for Best Supporting Actor for his performance in *How Green Was My Valley* in 1941.

La Rocque had been recently married to Vilma Banky, one of the biggest stars of the silent film era. Banky, who was publicized as the most beautiful woman in the world, was the Grace Kelly of her day, blonde, elegant, almost regal. La Rocque fell in love with her the first time they met. Banky was Hungarian and La Rocque wasn't certain how well she spoke

English. He went to a friend who spoke Hungarian and asked him how to say, "I love you." When he expressed his love to Banky in Hungarian, she laughed. She explained to him in English that he had just told her to "Go to hell." Despite their rude introduction, the two fell in love and were soon married. Banky, because of her thick Hungarian accent, was a casualty of sound pictures and she retired gracefully from acting, later making a fortune in real estate. Unlike most Hollywood marriages, theirs was a long and happy one. (Banky died in obscurity in 1991.)

In *Stand and Deliver*, Lupe played Jania, a Greek peasant girl rescued from a burning house by a soldier, Roger Norman (La Rocque). Later he is forced to kill his superior officer when the latter tries to rape Lupe. The pair is forced to flee to the mountains where they are captured by Chika. La Rocque escapes and becomes a hero when he saves the village from a bandit attack. Naturally, Lupe and La Rocque fall in love.

Stand and Deliver, a silent film with added sound effects, was a moderate success, more notable for Lupe's revealing outfits than for its acting. This was the film which earned Lupe the reputation as Hollywood's champion chest-heaver. *New York Times* film critic Mordaunt Hall wrote: "The exaggerated panting of Miss Velez during the supposedly agonizing moments may be excused by the nature of the story."

Lupe Velez was selected as one of the WAMPAS Baby Stars of 1928. Each year the Western Association of Motion Picture Advertisers selected the most promising new actresses of the year and honored them as "baby" stars. Sometimes the actresses were dressed in baby outfits to publicize the event.

In 1929, Lupe was cast in her most prestigious film to date, a lavish D. W. Griffith costume drama called *Lady of the Pavements*. The legendary director, often cited as the "father of the motion picture," was nearing the end of his distinguished career: Griffith, a sixth grade dropout, had wanted to be a playwright. His father, "Roaring" Jack Griffith was a Civil War hero. Unsuccessful as a playwright, Griffith accepted $5 a day as a bit player at the Biograph Studio. In 1908 he directed his first movie and his innovative techniques, such as close-ups and cross-cutting, revolutionized the ways films were made.

He had a great eye for talent, and discovered many screen legends including Lillian Gish and Mary Pickford. In 1915, Griffith directed *The Birth of a Nation* which earned millions of dollars and was considered the screen's first masterpiece. It had the distinction of being the first film shown at the White House and so impressed President Woodrow Wilson that he said, "It was like writing history with lightning." The film was controversial because Griffith, a Southerner, made the Ku Klux Klan the heroes of the film. The Klan was so pleased with their positive image that they used *The Birth of a Nation* as their official recruiting film.

The next year Griffith directed his greatest film, *Intolerance*. The film, which told four separate stories simultaneously, was Griffith's plea against intolerance throughout history. The scope of the film was enormous and the Babylonian scenes are still unmatched in their epic grandeur. Griffith poured the profits he had made from *The Birth of a Nation* into the film and while *Intolerance* was a critical success, it was a commercial disaster. Griffith continued to make noteworthy films such as *Broken Blossoms* and *Way Down East*, but by the time he made *Lady of the Pavements* he was considered a has-been. Originally, screenwriter Sam Taylor was supposed to direct the film, but was unavailable. Producer Joseph Schenck chose Griffith as a last minute replacement, hoping that teaming him with the red-hot Lupe Velez might revive his career.

Lupe's costar was William Boyd who had made his reputation appearing in a number of Cecil B. De Mille films. In those days, Boyd was a compulsive gambler and considered a playboy. Only in his thirties, his hair had turned prematurely silver.

Boyd appeared headed for superstardom when a case of mistaken identity sidetracked his career. In 1932, three years after starring in *Lady of the Pavements*, newspapers around the country carried a story that William Boyd had been booked on possession of illegal drugs and gambling equipment. According to the story, Boyd may have also been involved in a sex orgy. Boyd's photo accompanied the story. Only later was it discovered that the person who was arrested was a lesser-known Broadway actor with the same name. The damage was done and RKO released Boyd from his contract.

Unfairly, Boyd was relegated to B movies. In 1935, he was offered the lead in a western, *Hopalong Cassidy*. Incredibly, the first choice for the role had been a young English actor named David Niven. Boyd had been originally cast as the villain. To everyone's surprise, the character became extremely popular and Boyd went on to make 65 Hopalong Cassidy features (54 in a 8 year span) as well as a successful television series. At first Boyd was a terrible horseman but eventually he became an expert rider. In 1952 alone over 70 million dollars in Hopalong Cassidy merchandise was sold and by the time William Boyd retired he was a multi-millionaire.

In *Lady of the Pavements* Lupe played Nanon del Rayon, a singer at the Smoking Dog Cafe in Paris. Count Karl von Arnim (Boyd) tells a haughty and unfaithful countess (Jetta Goudal) that he would rather marry a woman of the streets than her. Deciding to teach him a lesson, the countess tricks him into falling in love with cafe soubrette Nanon disguised as a girl from the convent. As in *Pygmalion,* she is taught how to be socially acceptable. The transformation was less than perfect with Nanon's rough edges showing at the most inopportune times. As hoped, the count falls in love with the chanteuse but when the countess reveals Nanon's true identity he still accepts her for what she is.

Lupe's scenes as the chanteuse in the Smoking Dog Cafe were the liveliest in the film. Her short skirts complemented her shapely figure and Lupe's passionate thirty-second kisses with William Boyd caused a sensation. For the first time she was given the opportunity to display her fine singing voice. Irving Berlin had written several songs for Lupe including "Where Is That Song of Songs for Me" and "At the Dance." He had agreed to write the score for the film out of respect for D. W. Griffith. Berlin was born in Siberia and, after he came to America, sang for pennies on streetcorners on the Lower East Side of New York. He sold his first song for 37 cents. In 1911, his composition, "Alexander's Ragtime Band," made him world famous. During his long and illustrious career, Berlin wrote over

1,000 songs including standards such as "God Bless America," "Easter Parade," "There's No Business Like Show Business," and "White Christmas." His accomplishments were amazing when you consider that he was only able to write music in the key of F-sharp and needed to use a transposer device connected to his piano.

Berlin hated to be associated with flops and when word got out that *Lady of the Pavements* had its problems, he distanced himself from the film. It became apparent that it was in serious trouble at the world premier on January 22, 1929, at the United Artists Theater in Los Angeles. One of the major problems was Griffith's experimental use of sound. He tried, unsuccessfully, to vary the volume of the sound. The premier was a disaster.

Joe Schenck devised an ingenious plan to try to save the film. He sent Lupe Velez on a cross-country tour to bring out the crowds for the movie before the word got out how bad the film was. *Lady of the Pavements* had its Broadway opening at the Rialto Theater in March. Lupe was scheduled to perform four shows daily and her appearances clearly overshadowed the film. Headlines in the New York newspapers proclaimed that "Whoopee Lupe has threatened to paint the town red before she goes back to Hollywood."

Critic Richard Watts barely mentioned the film at all in his review in the *New York Post*, preferring to concentrate on Lupe's stage performance. "It is something of an indication of the new star's value that she receives so much space in the review of a photoplay directed by the distinguished D. W. Griffith."

Mordaunt Hall was also enthralled with Lupe, writing in *The New York Times*, "In the film Miss Velez is most suitably cast. She gives a clever performance as a Spanish dancer and singer in a Parisian cabaret known as Le Chien Qui Fume. She is far more apt to bite the hands of her masculine admirers than to caress or kiss them."

Hall also devoted more time to describing Lupe's stage act than to reviewing the film. "Miss Velez is appearing in person before the picture four times a day. She is a fascinating, vivacious, and resourceful little person who was not in the least dismayed yesterday by a few thousand persons in the audience. In fact, her songs and chatter were far more entertaining than all but a few of the Hollywood luminaries who have taken the stage before their films were offered. Miss Velez has a ready wit and her limited knowledge of English was never embarrassing for her, for if she was at a loss for a phrase she filled the gap with apt colloquialisms. She mimicked her rival in *Lady of the Pavements*, Jetta Goudal, also Gloria Swanson and Dolores Del Rio, much to the delight of those who packed the theater."

Lupe took particular pleasure in her mimicry of Goudal, her statuesque costar in the film. The rivalry between the two women began when Griffith built up Lupe's part at the expense of temperamental Goudal, with whom he did not get along. Crowds continued to return daily, mainly to see Lupe's show, although many in the audience had difficulty understanding her broken English. It became a fashionable game in New York to see who in the audience could understand the most of what Lupe was saying.

Critics were less kind to the film, in particular to its director, D. W. Griffith. A review in the *New York Sun* was typical of the response: "Mr. Griffith has turned

[Lupe's] animalism into cuteness. He has done her hair into little pompadours, made her pigeon-toed, and rather coy, and when she begins to upset court functions, one is reminded of the gosling days of the Gishes and Dempsters."

The failure of the film and being overshadowed by Lupe Velez were final humiliations for Griffith. He directed only two more films then went into seclusion, a broken man. Shortly before Griffith's death in 1948 at age seventy-three, a journalist interviewed him in his hotel room and wrote sadly, "The father of the American film sat in an easy chair in a hotel room guzzling gin out of a water glass."

United Artists, Lupe's studio, wrote a clause into her contract which forbade her from indulging in strenuous diets or reducing exercises which might affect her curvaceous figure. They needn't have worried. Lupe had a voracious appetite but she never seemed to gain a pound.

Lupe's new love was a Russ Columbo, a handsome young crooner with wavy black hair. One of ten children, he was born Ruggerio Eugenio di Rudolpho Colombo in 1908. He bore a striking resemblance to Rudolph Valentino and women found him irresistible. Columbo was very vain about his looks and spent large sums of money each week on expensive hair and sunlamp treatments. He carried a mirror in his pocket and often removed it to admire his handsome image.

Columbo literally worshipped the women he loved and millions in return worshipped the sexy baritone. When he rolled his eyes while singing a love song every woman present believed he was singing to her. Columbo's big break came in 1928 when he sang duets with Bing Crosby at the Cocoanut Grove in Los Angeles. By the time he was twenty years old, he was a national sensation.

Like many of her relationships, Lupe's affair with Russ Columbo was brief and intense. Columbo appeared on his way to becoming one of the biggest stars in show business. He had a long string of hits including "Too Beautiful For Words," "Let's Pretend There's a Moon," "When You're in Love," "You've Captured My Heart," and his signature song, "Prisoner of Love." And he had a friendly rivalry with Bing Crosby which was known as the "Battle of the Baritones."

Russ Columbo made his film debut in *Wolf Song*, which starred Gary Cooper and Lupe Velez, and was directed by Victor Fleming. Here in one picture were three of Lupe's lovers: past (Columbo), present (Fleming), and future (Cooper).

Columbo's career continued to prosper after his subsequent breakup with Lupe. His personal appearance tours were sold out from coast-to-coast. NBC gave him his own radio program and it was so successful that he became known as the "Romeo of Song" and the "Radio Valentino." Columbo opened his own nightspot, the Club Pyramid, on Santa Monica Boulevard and formed his own record publishing company. Universal Studios signed him to a long-term film contract. His career was at its zenith when tragedy struck. On September 1, 1934, Columbo visited his best friend, photographer Lansing Brown. Brown was showing Columbo his collection of Civil War dueling pistols when one of the guns accidentally fired. The bullet ricocheted off a desk and struck Columbo in the left eye and lodged in his brain. He died two hours later at the hospital. Russ Columbo was only twenty-six.

There was a bizarre aftermath to Columbo's death.

Two days before Columbo was shot, his blind mother had a serious heart attack. The family was concerned that if they told her of Russ' death that the shock might be too much for her heart. At Carole Lombard's suggestion, they concocted a plan to keep the news from her. For the last ten years of her life, the family read her spurious letters from Russ which assured her how well his career was going. The deception was so successful that when she died, Russ' mother left part of her estate to him in her will.

One of the main reasons for Lupe's breakup with Russ Columbo was her new romance with Victor Fleming, one of Hollywood's top directors, and the man who called the shots on *Wolf Song*. Whereas Columbo worshipped women, Fleming had the reputation of being a man's man.

Fleming entered the movies by accident. He was working as a mechanic in 1911 when Allan Dwan, one of Hollywood's pioneer directors, hired him to fix his car. He did such a good job that Dwan offered him a job in the movies as a cameraman's assistant. Soon he bluffed his way into becoming the head of photography at Triangle Studio. For a time he supplemented his income by working as Douglas Fairbanks' chauffeur. It was Douglas Fairbanks who, in 1919, offered him his first director's job.

Nicknamed the "Mad Monk," Fleming quickly established his reputation as a tough guy. He loved to race automobiles and motorcycles. Allan Dwan noted, "He loved to fight and drink." Fleming's daughter, Victoria, called him "a cross between [Generals] Patton and MacArthur."

Clark Gable admitted that he based his masculine screen persona on his good friend, Victor Fleming. In the late 1930's Gable and Fleming were members of an overage motorcycle gang called the Morango Spit & Polish Club. When George Cukor was named to direct *Gone With the Wind*, Gable insisted on Fleming. Cukor was known as a woman's director and was a homosexual. Fearing that Vivien Leigh would be allowed to dominate the film, Gable told the producer, "Look, this picture calls for a man." At the King's insistence Cukor was replaced with Fleming.

Fleming also developed a reputation as a ladies' man, which was unsurpassed in Hollywood. Columbia Pictures head Harry Cohn observed, "He was positively irresistible to women. He had an overwhelming male charisma." Director Henry Hathaway remarked, "Every dame he worked with fell on her ass for him." Sometimes this was literally true. Fleming frequently slapped actresses during filming; Judy Garland, Lana Turner, and Ingrid Bergman all felt the sting from the back of his hand. Ingrid Bergman recalled that during the shooting of *Dr. Jekyll and Mr. Hyde*, Fleming slapped her across the face backwards and forwards so she would become hysterical during a scene. Instantly, Bergman burst into tears. Fleming, having achieved the effect he desired, yelled, "Action!" Bergman, like almost every other woman he ever knew, fell in love with Fleming who was 64 years old at the time but still attractive.

Fleming's stepdaughter, Helen Rosen, described his macho appeal, "Women just fell all over themselves to get at him, he was so attractive: six feet tall and perfectly proportioned, with steel gray eyes, salt-and-pepper hair, and a deep voice."

One of his early conquests was Norma Shearer, who fell in love with him during the filming of *Empty Hands* in 1924. Their affair helped publicize his sexual prowess. His most notorious affair was with the "It" girl, Clara Bow. Fleming directed Bow in two of her biggest hits, *Mantrap* and *Hula*. Her nude swimming scene in the latter created a sensation.

It was inevitable that these two prodigious lovers would have an affair. Bow, whose promiscuity has become legendary, told a friend that Victor Fleming was the great love of her life. As good a lover as Fleming was, he was unable to satisfy the insatiable Clara who demanded a paramour who could go all night. After making love to Fleming, Clara would go off, presumably to another lover. When the relationship ended Clara sighed, "He's not so much fun anymore."

Lupe Velez disagreed. Victor Fleming would not be the last of Clara Bow's pass-me-down lovers. At forty-four, Fleming was old enough to be Lupe's father but temperamentally they were ideally suited to one another. Both had an incredible zest for life and both loved to fight. Under different circumstances, their relationship might have been a lasting one. However, someone was about to enter Lupe's life who would make her forget all about Victor Fleming.

5

The Greatest Cocksman
That Ever Lived

Victor Fleming used his influence at the studio to secure the best roles he could for Lupe. They decided to work together on their next film, *Wolf Song* (1929). Lupe's costar was the young actor who had already acquired the reputation as being the biggest stud in town, Gary Cooper. The love affair of Lupe Velez and Gary Cooper was one of Hollywood's most passionate and turbulent. By the time their affair ended three years later, Cooper had to flee to Europe to recover from a nervous breakdown. He had never met a woman like Lupe Velez.

The son of the Chief Justice of the Montana Supreme Court, Cooper moved to California in 1924, hoping for a career as a cartoonist. Both of his parents were British and Cooper spent three years in an English prep school. Cooper arrived in Hollywood with $100 in his pocket and spent five months working as a milkman. Soon, because of his expert horsemanship, he began earning $3 a day as a movie extra. The studio showed little interest in Cooper and he had to pay $65 for a screen test which consisted of him riding a horse and smiling at the camera. In those days, Cooper used his real name, Frank. Since there was already another actor named Frank Cooper his agent, Nan Collins, decided to change his name to Gary, after her hometown in Indiana. Cooper joked, "It was a good thing she didn't come from Poughkeepsie."

Cooper's acting career may never have gotten off the ground were it not for the intervention of Brooklyn-born Clara Bow, the most popular female star of the twenties. Known as the "It" girl, she personified the anything goes attitude of the flapper. Born in Brooklyn, Clara overcame a tragic childhood. At the age of five she witnessed the death of her grandfather who had a stroke while he was pushing her in a swing. Three years later, a young playmate died in her arms after he had been burned in a fire.

In 1921, when she was sixteen, Clara won the nation-wide "Fame and Fortune" Contest sponsored by Motion Picture Magazine to find the most beautiful girl in the world. As the winner, she earned a trip to Holly-wood and a chance to appear in a movie. Her mentally unstable mother opposed her ambition to be an ac-tress. One night Clara awoke with her mother holding a butcher knife to her throat. "You're going straight to hell. I'd rather see you dead than be an actress," her mother shrieked. Terrified, Clara escaped to the bath-room and locked herself in. For the rest of her life Clara suffered from insomnia.

Her mother was committed to a mental institution where she died shortly thereafter. The distraught Clara threw herself into her mother's open grave. Clara Bow went to Hollywood and the movie industry took note of her flaming red hair, bee stung lips, and a figure described as luscious. She became Paramount's biggest star; in 1925 alone she starred in 14 films. Author Elinor Glyn dubbed her the "It Girl." Glyn defined "It" as a "strange magnetism which attracted both sexes." Actress Louise Brooks, herself a major star during the period, said, "Clara Bow was the twenties."

Clara certainly attracted members of the male sex. Her close encounter with death had made her determined to live life to the fullest. She vowed, "to snatch every moment of fun and excitement." Clara had a legion of lovers including Victor Fleming, Gilbert Roland, John Gilbert, Richard Arlen, Buddy Rogers, Fredric March, and Eddie Cantor. She also had a rather strange relationship with Bela Lugosi, who later became famous playing Dracula. Lugosi kept a nude photo of Bow in his house for years after their affair ended.

The incident with her knife-wielding mother had given Clara a fear of sleeping. Her favorite way of passing the long nighttime hours was to make love. Screenwriter Anita Loos, author of *Gentlemen Prefer Blondes*, called her the biggest tramp in Hollywood. The most intriguing story about Clara's promiscuity was that she once slept with the entire 1927 University of Southern California Trojans football team. Neighbors complained that they witnessed nude football games on Bow's lawn. During the filming of Wings she skillfully manipulated three lovers at the same time. Director William Wellman marveled, "They were handled like chessmen, never running into one another."

Bow was literally a femme fatale. Yale football star, Robert Savage, confessed that Clara kissed him so hard that his lips bled. When she refused to marry him, Savage slashed his wrists, letting his blood drip on her photo. When Clara learned of her lover's fate she said, "He's got to be kidding. Men don't slash their wrists, they use a gun!"

Gary Cooper was working as a stunt man when he met Clara. She was overwhelmed by the tall, handsome Cooper and they became lovers. They made love whenever and wherever they could—in walnut groves, swimming pools, on the beach, or in the backseat of a car. Cooper had remarkable sexual staying power and was the first of Clara's lovers who could match her in bed. She confided to her close friend, Hedda Hopper, "He was hung like a horse and could go all night."

Clara convinced the studio to give Cooper parts in *It* and *Wings,* two of her biggest hits. She used her influenced to get him his first starring role opposite her in *Children of Divorce.* Cooper was so nervous that his legs shook noticeably and director Frank Lloyd had to shoot all of his scenes from the waist up. Although a great lover offscreen, Cooper was so uncomfortable in his love scenes with Bow that he fled from the set. Cooper drove down Highway 101 to the desert, certain that his acting career was over. It took Frank Lloyd several days to locate Cooper and to convince him to return to the set.

Hedda Hopper, then still an actress, suggested to Clara that the best way to give Cooper confidence was to have him serve as her public escort. The two were seen everywhere. Clara liked to drive down Sunset Boulevard in her red Kissel convertible. In the back seat she kept her seven Chows and a monkey, all dyed bright red to match her hair.

As a result of his exposure on Clara Bow's arm, Gary Cooper became a household name. He began to be known around Hollywood as the "It Boy," a nickname he detested. Cooper was not above using women, however, to further his career. "It happens that I have made friendships with women who have aided me in my work and that they have been happy contacts. It was that way with Clara."

With the coming of sound, Cooper's career was on the rise while Bow's was on the decline. The roaring twenties were drawing to a close and Clara's jazz baby image had become passé. Her Brooklyn accent became a liability in talkies but it was a series of scandals which wrecked her career.

Dr. William Pearson, a Texas physician, rubbed love balm on Clara nightly. His wife sued Bow for $30,000 for alienation-of-affections and the public began to learn about her active sex life. The real scandal occurred when Clara discovered that her trusted private secretary, Daisy DeVoe, had embezzled $16,000 of her money. When she pressed charges, DeVoe revealed to a tabloid details about Clara's prolific sex life.

DeVoe was convicted of the charges and sentenced to 18 months in jail. However, Clara Bow was really the person on trial. The strain of the ordeal resulted in her first nervous breakdown and she was placed in a sanitarium in Glendale. That was it for the "It girl."

A has-been at age twenty-four, Clara Bow retired from the screen in 1933. She married cowboy star Rex Bell and lived on a ranch in Nevada where she dyed the cows red. In and out of sanitariums for the remainder of her life, she sent Christmas cards to her friends each year signed, "Remember me? Clara Bow." In 1965, still unable to sleep, she died of a heart attack while watching a late night movie on television.

Gary Cooper cleverly distanced himself from the Clara's scandals by declaring that their relationship was merely a publicity stunt. One of his first films following his split with her was *Wolf Song* with Lupe Velez. Lupe's salary of $2,500 per week was more than three times Cooper's.

The attraction between Lupe Velez and Gary Cooper was instantaneous; they slept together the first night they met. Victor Fleming, who had previously lost Clara Bow to Cooper, watched helplessly as the same thing happened with Lupe Velez. It was a classic example of opposites attracting. Lupe was tiny and talkative; Gary was tall and laconic.

Adela Rogers St. Johns wrote: "It seemed so funny, tiny, tempestuous Lupe and six-foot-three of slow-moving Cooper; her firecracker Mexican accent and her sparkling laughter against the slow drawl and slower smile of the big cowboy; Lupe's public demonstration and declarations of love and Gary's embarrassment and adoration."

The one thing Lupe and Gary shared was an almost animalistic approach to lovemaking. Cooper told *Photoplay*: "In Lupe Velez, I find a girl who takes the same joy out of primitive, elemental things that I do."

Director Stuart Heisler described Cooper's appeal: "Coop was probably the greatest cocksman that ever lived. They fell over themselves to get him to take them to bed. He couldn't stop screwing around. The women wouldn't let him. They'd go lay down for him in a portable dressing room by the soundstage. I guess he had the reputation for being a wonderful lay."

Howard Hawks, the director of such classics as Scarface, *Bringing Up Baby*, and *His Girl Friday*, observed Cooper's seduction technique: "If I ever saw him with a good-looking girl and he was kind of dragging his feet over the ground and being very shy and looking down, I'd say, 'Oh-oh, the snake's going to strike again. He found that the little bashful boy approach was very successful."

Lupe gave a mixed review of Cooper's lovemaking abilities. "He has the biggest organ in Hollywood but not the ass to push it in well."

Adela Rogers St. Johns wrote, "Lupe Velez hit Gary Cooper like a Mexican thunderstorm." Cooper began to show the effects of his wild nights with Lupe. During the filming of *Wolf Song*, he kept falling asleep on the set but he always managed to wake up for his love scenes with Lupe.

"I guess I was in love with Velez as much as one could get with a creature as elusive as quicksilver," Cooper wrote years later. "You couldn't help being attracted to Lupe Velez. She flashed, stormed, and sparked, and on the set she was apt to throw things if she thought it would do any good. But she objected to being called wild. She'd say, 'I am not wild! I am just Lupe.' "

Lupe took Cooper to Clark Gable's ex-wife, Josephine Dillon, the renowned drama coach, for acting lessons. It was Dillon who had helped Lupe with her acting and her English—though not too well in the latter area.

Cooper really didn't need the acting lessons; he was a natural. John Barrymore said of Cooper, "That fellow is the world's greatest actor. He can do with no effort, what the rest of us spent years trying to learn: be perfectly natural."

Wolf Song was shot on location in the California

Sierras. The film, which was set at the time of the Gold Rush, was a part-talkie with limited dialogue. Lupe sang two songs: "Mi Amado" and "Yo Te Amo Means I Love You."

Lupe plays Lola Salazar, the highborn daughter of a California don, and Cooper portrays Sam Lash, a Kentucky trapper, who courts the high-spirited girl. They elope to the mountains where they are married. Their happiness is short-lived as he heeds to the wolf song and returns to his solitary way of life. After he is ambushed and wounded by Indians he is reunited with Lupe.

Lupe Velez was instrumental in the launching of the career of famed Hollywood costume designer, Edith Head, who was a young assistant designer on *Wolf Song*. Initially, Lupe was insulted that an inexperienced assistant was put in charge of her wardrobe. She wanted to look especially beautiful in her love scenes with Cooper and demanded lavish costumes. Edith Head created a gorgeous white billowing lace gown which delighted Lupe. Her reputation was established and Head over the years became the most celebrated costume designer in film.

In her biography, Head recalled getting into an argument with director Victor Fleming on how revealing Lupe's costumes should be: "In covered wagon days, ladies wore high collars. But Victor Fleming, the director, wanted Lupe to be so sexy that most of the time her bosom would be hanging out. I went to Mr. Fleming and said, 'Don't you think that it's a little inconsistent? Women did not uncover their bosom in those days.' He told me, 'Edith, if no woman had ever shown her bosom in those days, you wouldn't be here.'"

Wolf Song was released in February 1929 to mixed reviews. Mordaunt Hall wrote, "That exotic and curiously attractive Mexican actress, Lupe Velez, who achieved no little distinction by her interpretation of a termagant in Douglas Fairbanks' production of *The Gaucho*, is now seen as a more placid young woman in *Wolf Song*." Not expanding on the probably widely known fact that the pair wasn't acting, Hall noted: "Velez and Cooper prolonged a violent kiss until it became more absurd than passionate."

Motion Picture News found: "Lupe Velez indulges in a flock of respiratory aerobatics whenever she has a love scene with Gary. Lupe's voice is pleasing enough but she is difficult to understand." *Variety* concurred: "As a chest-heaver, Lupe's a champ."

Wolf Song turned into a box-office smash, mainly because of the publicity generated by the torrid Velez-Cooper romance. "Lupe Velez didn't object to the publicity, figuring it to be good box office," Cooper remembered. "She had come up the hard way, using every ounce of her vitality and vivacity to make it."

Lupe and Gary toured the country, drawing large crowds wherever they appeared. Cooper explained, "The depression hit pretty hard and people needed romance. Seeing us in love on the screen and then in person was proof that movies are not all make-believe."

When they returned to Hollywood, Cooper moved into Velez's Laurel Canyon hideaway. Cooper was twenty-eight years old but he was still living with his parents. Fan magazines ran stories about the couple, and they were photographed everywhere they went — at premieres, nightclubs, and restaurants. Author F. Scott Fitzgerald told about once being pushed aside by a photographer at a Hollywood nightclub when Gary Cooper and Lupe Velez arrived. Cooper recalled, "The most casual linking of our names caused dynamite."

At first Velez and Cooper were inseparable. Lupe spent over $400 a month on long distance phone calls to Cooper when she was away from Hollywood. "If I do not speak to him I will die," she confessed. "I am so lonesome for him."

Many of the telephone calls were of a highly erotic nature. Cooper received most of them in his dressing room. He had the unusual habit of wearing no clothes when he was in his dressing room, a practice which made it easier for him to have sex between takes. Whenever Lupe called, Cooper reportedly had an erection during the conversation as she described, in great detail, how she would make love to him the next time they were together.

In February 1929, Cooper accompanied Velez to the Santa Fe Railroad Station in Pasadena. Lupe flashed a ring to reporters, fueling speculation that the couple were engaged. A *Los Angeles Times* reporter described the departure:

"The scene at the station will not easily be forgotten. In that last frantic moment of good-bye, not being able to open the window to give Gary another farewell kiss, Lupe decided the thing to do was to break the window. She had to be physically restrained from breaking the glass."

A few years later there would be another farewell at a railroad station but the circumstances would be quite different.

6

Jack Dempsey and Jack Johnson

Only twenty years old, Lupe was at the peak of her popularity. United Artists realized that she was a valuable property and loaned her to other studios. In 1929, she was borrowed by Metro-Goldwyn-Mayer for *Where East Is East* with Lon Chaney. Known as "The Man of a Thousand Faces," Chaney was the first actor to master the use of makeup and almost single-handedly invented the horror genre.

Chaney, born to deaf parents, worked as a guide on Pikes' Peak as a child. He began in show business as a comedian and, because of his expertise with make-up, became a clown. His first wife, singer Cleva Creighton, was more famous than Chaney at the time, however, her career was jeopardized by her heavy drinking. After a quarrel, she attempted suicide by swallowing poison on stage during his act. She survived but the poison burned away her vocal chords and destroyed her singing career.

Chaney divorced Creighton and married Hazel Hastings, a chorus girl who left her husband, a double amputee. Oddly, Chaney established his reputation in films portraying cripples, hunchbacks, dope addicts, phantoms, and mad scientists. He created some of the most memorable characters in silent film such as Quasimodo, the Hunchback of Notre Dame, and the Phantom of the Opera. The unmasking of his phantom is still one of the most frightening moments in film history.

Sadly, Chaney learned that he had throat cancer shortly after completing *Where East Is East*. He had been scheduled to next play Dracula, but when his illness prevented this, the part went to Bela Lugosi and it made him a star. Lon Chaney died in 1930 but his son Creighton changed his name to Lon Chaney, Jr., and carried on the family tradition in horror films such as *The Wolf Man*.

The director of *Where East Is East*, Tod Browning, directed Chaney in several classic silents. Before entering films, Browning had worked on a variety of unusual jobs including being a contortionist and a circus performer. Probably his strangest occupation was appearing as the "Living Hypnotic Corpse" in riverboat shows.

He was introduced to D. W. Griffith who cast him as an undertaker in one of his films. Browning soon gave up acting for directing and established himself as the master of the horror genre. After Chaney's death, Browning directed his two most famous films, *Dracula* (1931) and *Freaks* (1932). The latter film used actual circus freaks and was so disturbing that it was withdrawn shortly after its release and not shown again for 30 years.

Where East Is East is set in Indochina where Lupe plays Toyo, the half-caste daughter of a wild animal trapper, Tiger Haynes (Lon Chaney), whose face is horribly disfigured by tiger claw scars. Bobby Bailey (Lloyd Hughes), the handsome son of an American circus owner, falls in love with Lupe and asks for permission to marry her. Haynes' ex-wife, the exotic Madame de Sylva (Estelle Taylor), seduces Toyo's fiancé. In retaliation, Haynes unleashes a killer gorilla which not only dispatches Madame de Sylva but also mortally wounds him. Toyo and repentant Bailey are now free to marry.

Estelle Taylor, who played the wicked Madame de Sylva, became Lupe's closest friend. The shapely brunette with the beautiful face and sharp tongue had married a banker when she was only fourteen. After winning a beauty contest, she came to Hollywood in 1922, and the following year she appeared in Cecil B. DeMille's *The Ten Commandments.* Taylor became a star in 1926 when she portrayed Lucrezia Borgia opposite John Barrymore in *Don Juan.*

The beautiful Taylor attracted many Hollywood leading men including Charlie Chaplin. When a reporter asked her if she was engaged to Chaplin, she retorted, "No, I couldn't take that kind of punishment. I will pick my own persimmons. Charlie isn't one of them."

The persimmon she picked was heavyweight champion Jack Dempsey. In the ring Dempsey couldn't be gotten off his feet but he fell hard for Estelle Taylor.

Dempsey had won the heavyweight title in 1919 when he knocked out Jess Willard in the third round. Dempsey gave six-foot-six Willard a savage beating, sending the champ to the canvas seven times and breaking his jaw. The damage to Willard's face was so severe that it was rumored that Dempsey had wrapped his hands in plaster of Paris. Throughout the 1920s he defeated all comers including Georges "The Orchid Man" Carpentier and Luis "The Wild Bull of the Pampas" Firpo.

On the spur of the moment, after a day at the Tijuana Racetrack, Jack Dempsey and Estelle Taylor were married. It seemed as though they had absolutely nothing in common. Dempsey wanted Estelle to give up her acting career and she refused. She despised boxing and encouraged him to retire. He was so smitten with Estelle that he announced that he was going to give up boxing and become a hotel manager. Dempsey hated Taylor's Hollywood friends and she refused to associate with the pugs he hung out with.

Dempsey admitted that he loved Estelle Taylor "too terribly" and she began to tame the "Manassa Mauler." The bedroom of their home was draped with silk and satin and they slept on lace covered pillows. When they traveled abroad, Estelle insisted on having a large dog. Dempsey reluctantly bought her a three-hundred pound blue hoarhound named Castor. The great hound, which author Gene Fowler described as looking like the Abominable Snowman, caused $10,000 damage in a Paris hotel, mauled an unfortunate Airedale to death, and broke the arm of its handler. Finally, Dempsey had to pay someone to take the hound from hell off his hands.

None of this pleased Doc Kearns, Dempsey's boxing manager, who disliked Estelle Taylor from the start and did not appreciate her efforts to domesticate his champ. Estelle in turn did everything in her power to get rid of Kearns. Kearns threatened Estelle by telling her he had unearthed some scandalous things in her past and he would tell Dempsey and the press if she didn't divorce him. In 1926, their animosity came out in an ugly incident at the Montmartre Cafe in Hollywood. Forced to choose between his beautiful wife and the man who had guided him to the heavyweight championship, Dempsey chose Estelle.

At Estelle's insistence, Dempsey had not gotten into the ring since they were married. He had not defended his title in three years and pressure was being put on him to fight an up-and-coming challenger named Gene Tunney. Tunney, the former light heavyweight champion, had lost only one match—to a one-eyed fighter named Harry Greb, who would sometimes remove his glass eye during a fight to startle an opponent. Sometimes his opponent was so surprised that Greb was able to knock out his distracted foe. Reportedly, Dempsey was terrified of Greb and his glass eye and refused to fight him.

The Dempsey-Tunney fight was scheduled for Philadelphia on September 23, 1926. The strain of his marriage to Estelle Taylor had taken its toll on his once magnificent body. His skin was cracking, due to dermatitis caused by stress. His pores were affected and he had difficulty sweating, causing his body to overheat. He drank olive oil to calm his irritated digestive track. Without Kearns in his corner, Dempsey was no match for the quicker Tunney who outboxed him on the way to an unanimous decision. Estelle refused to attend the fight, locking herself in the bathroom until it was over.

A year later, more than 120,000 spectators attended the Dempsey-Tunney rematch in Chicago. In the seventh round Dempsey floored Tunney with a vicious combination. A new rule required the fighter to go to a neutral corner following a knockdown. Dempsey, who had always hovered over his fallen opponent, forgot to go to the corner and the referee didn't start counting until five seconds had elapsed. Tunney barely beat the count and recovered to win a ten-round decision.

The "long count" fight became part of boxing lore and Dempsey would never box again. Estelle encouraged him to try acting and they appeared together on Broadway in a play entitled *The Big Fight*. The title was an accurate description of their marriage which was swiftly deteriorating, thanks, in part, to Lupe Velez.

According to Dempsey, he and Lupe had a brief relationship prior to his meeting Estelle Taylor. He enjoyed Lupe's company but didn't feel they were right for each other. Lupe was stunned when Dempsey unexpectedly broke off their relationship, and she never forgave him. When he wed, she vowed to do whatever she could to break up the marriage.

Lupe constantly told Estelle Taylor that Dempsey wasn't good enough for her and warned her that being married to a prizefighter would ruin her career. When rumors began circulating that Dempsey was having an affair with a showgirl named Agnes O'Loughlin, Lupe fueled the speculation. Estelle Taylor believed everything Lupe told her. Dempsey tried to bar Lupe from his home but Estelle refused, arguing that Lupe was her best friend and would always be welcome. Things became violent when Dempsey, in a fit of rage and frustration, threw Estelle out of a window.

Finally, in 1930, Dempsey filed for divorce. In the courtroom his nemesis, Lupe, sat triumphantly next to Estelle during the proceedings. After the divorce was granted, Lupe told the press how happy she was for Estelle.

Throughout her life, Lupe had a thing for fighting and boxers. She had carried on a secret love affair with Jack Johnson, the controversial black former heavyweight champion. Boxing historian Nat Fleischer said, "I have no hesitation of naming Jack Johnson the greatest of them all." Johnson was the first fighter to raise boxing to a science, combining footwork, an elusive defense, and a persistent jab. Years later, another black fighter, Muhammad Ali, would emulate his style.

Like Ali, Johnson was always the center of controversy. As a young man he had participated in humiliating contests called battle royals. In those days most boxing matches were staged in private men's clubs. In the South, black fighters were forced to strip naked and were blindfolded. Wearing Sambo masks, the fighters would swing blindly at one another until only one was left standing. The spectator rewarded the winner by pelting the victor with loose change. Johnson never forgot the shame of the battle royals and swore that someday he would be the heavyweight champion of the world.

His goal seemed an impossibility at the time. It was considered unthinkable to give a black fighter a shot at the championship. Johnson turned professional in 1897 and six years later won the Negro heavyweight championship. His career received a setback in 1905 when he lost a decision to future champ, Marvin Hart. Two years later though became the top contender when he knocked out aging ex-champion Bob Fitzsimmons in two rounds. He set his sights on heavyweight champion Tommy Burns.

Johnson chased Burns all over the world, demanding a title shot. Burns evaded him for two years before agreeing to a fight to be held in Sydney, Australia, on December 26, 1908, on the condition that he (Burns) be permitted to select the referee. His choice was Hugh McIntosh, who was believed to also be serving as Burns' manager.

From the beginning of the bout it was apparent that the smaller Burns was no match for Johnson. At five-foot-seven and 175 pounds, Burns was the smallest heavyweight champion in history and half a foot shorter than Johnson. Before the fight Burns had called Johnson coon and nigger, and Johnson made the champion pay by taunting him throughout the fight and administering a brutal beating. In the fourteenth round the police jumped into the ring to stop the fight, fearing that if the crowd saw a black man knock out a white that there would be a riot. When news of Johnson's victory reached the United States, there *were* riots which resulted in nineteen deaths.

Once he became champion, Johnson's outlandish behavior infuriated white America. In public, he wore flashy clothes and carried a fancy gold-headed cane. Johnson had a diamond implanted in his gold capped teeth and drank wine through a gold straw. Johnson loved driving fast and expensive cars and said, "My mind is constantly on automobiles." His reckless driving made headlines but it was his preference for white women which outraged the public.

In his autobiography, *In the Ring and Out,* Johnson wrote, "There have been countless women in my life." Stories circulated about his incredible sexual prowess and the enormous size of his penis. In order to aggravate his detractors, he wore skin tight trunks and wrapped his penis in gauze to make it appear larger.

Johnson always contended that his preference for white women was simply because they treated him better. His first wife was black but she divorced him because he wouldn't give up boxing. His next girlfriend, also black, left him for a white man and ran off with all of his money. Distrustful of black women, Johnson always seemed to be surrounded by an entourage of young white women. Johnson defended his personal life, "I have the right to choose who my mate shall be without the dictation of any man. I have eyes and a heart and when they fail to tell me who I shall have for mine, I want to be put away in a lunatic asylum."

Johnson was a fighting champion, defending his title six times in 1909. In October, he signed to fight middleweight champion Stanley Ketchel, a brutal fighter known as the "Michigan Assassin." Ketchel, considered by many experts to be the greatest middleweight of all time, was a bloodthirsty fighter who enjoyed beating his opponents to a pulp. One sportswriter graphically described his menacing appearance, "A face like that cannot be manufactured by makeup artists. To find such a face search the insane asylums or the prison death house."

Despite being thirty pounds lighter, Ketchel held his

own with Johnson for eleven rounds. In the twelfth he stunned the crowd—and Johnson—when he knocked the champion down with a powerful right hand. Johnson shook off the effects of the punch and got to his feet. As Ketchel moved in for the kill, Johnson caught him with a tremendous right. Ketchel slumped to the canvas and was counted out. The blow was so hard that several of Ketchel's teeth lodged in Johnson's glove.

As Johnson's victory total grew there was a nationwide search for a white fighter who could put him in his place. Jim Jeffries, the popular undefeated former champion was urged to come out of retirement. Jeffries had retired to his California alfalfa farm five years earlier and his weight had ballooned to 320 pounds. He reluctantly became the "Great White Hope."

The fight took place on Independence Day, 1910, in San Francisco. Johnson, distrustful of the promoter, demanded to be paid $30,000 in $20 gold pieces. Jeffries had been a powerhouse in his prime but he hadn't fought in five years and it showed. Johnson taunted Jeffries as he pounded his older, slower opponent. At ringside, former champion "Gentleman Jim" Corbett made faces at Johnson in a pathetic attempt to distract him. In the fifteenth round Johnson sent Jeffries to the canvas three times and the mismatch was mercifully stopped. A gracious Jeffries acknowledged Johnson's skill when he said, "I could never have whipped Jack Johnson at my best. I couldn't have reached him in a thousand years."

When it became apparent that there were no boxers who could defeat Johnson, other means were devised. Johnson had married his first white wife, Etta Duryea, in 1909. He loved her dearly but she feared having

children and, for most of the marriage, slept in a separate bedroom. On September 11, 1912, she committed
suicide by shooting herself in the head. Two months
later, Johnson was indicted for a supposed violation of
the Mann Act. The trumped up charge alleged that he
had transported Belle Schreiber, a white woman whom
he lived with, across state lines for immoral purposes.
In 1913, the government indicted him on eleven
charges ranging from aiding prostitution to unlawful
sexual crimes against nature.

Sentenced to a year in prison, Johnson fled the coun-
try. He spent seven years in exile in Europe, South
America, and Cuba. In Europe he received the acclaim
never given in his own country. He had an affair with
Mata Hari, the beautiful and notorious Dutch spy of
World War I. He began wearing a beret and affected a
British accent.

Johnson continued to defend his title successfully all
over the world. In 1915, he signed to fight Jess Willard
in Havana. Willard, nicknamed the "Pottawatomie Giant," was six-foot-six and 250 pounds. He accomplished
what no one else had been able to do when he knocked
out Johnson in the twenty-sixth round. For the rest of
his life Johnson claimed that he had taken a dive as part
of a deal he had made with the United States government to allow him back into the country. As evidence,
he cited that he held his glove up to shield his eyes
from the sun while he was being counted out.

He continued to box, but never again had a chance
to fight for the title. In 1920, Johnson returned to the
United States and served one year in Leavenworth.
Even in prison he continued to fight, winning all five
matches.

Johnson was nearly fifty years old when he met Lupe. He was still fighting because years of high living and legal expenses had depleted his savings. Johnson was still a striking presence with his shaved bullet-shaped head and his powerful physique. Their torrid affair was kept secret because, at the time, revelations about an interracial romance would have probably destroyed Lupe's career.

Johnson retired from boxing in 1928. His later years were spent in a variety of demeaning jobs. During his final years he appeared as a sideshow attraction at a dime museum and flea circus in New York. Standing on a three-foot platform and wearing a bright red tie and blue beret, Johnson recited the story of his colorful life. To make the task bearable, he used his imagination to fabricate a different story every day.

Johnson never lost his love for fast cars. On June 10, 1946, while he was driving on Highway 1 near Raleigh, North Carolina, en route to see the second Joe Louis-Billy Conn heavyweight championship fight, his Lincoln Zephyr swerved to avoid a truck, and hit a pole. Johnson was killed when he was thrown from the wreckage. Although he had been heavyweight champion for seven years, no one from the boxing world attended his funeral.

7

Sex Was Her Game

In 1929, Lupe starred in her first all-talking picture, *Tiger Rose*, opposite Monte Blue, a favorite actor of directors D. W. Griffith and Ernst Lubitsch. Tall, with a dour disposition, Blue had worked as a gravedigger, cowhand, reporter, and circus bareback rider before breaking into movies as a stuntman for Griffith. Blue appeared in many classic silent films including *The Birth of a Nation, Intolerance,* and *The Marriage Circle*.

The real star of *Tiger Rose* was Rin-Tin-Tin. The German Shepherd was discovered in a trench during World War I by Captain Lee Duncan. Brought to Hollywood, Rin-Tin-Tin made his film debut in *The Man From Hells River* in 1922, and for the next decade was Warner Brothers' biggest moneymaker, virtually saving the studio from bankruptcy. The dog was so important that future studio head Darryl F. Zanuck personally wrote the scripts for his movies.

In *Tiger Rose* Lupe plays the title character, a tempestuous French Canadian half-caste. It seems as though she is being pursued by every man north of the border, in particular a Royal Canadian Mountie named Devlin (Monte Blue). Rose loves Bruce (Grant Withers) a young railroad engineer who accidentally kills a deranged doctor (H.B. Warner). Devlin tracks down Bruce with the help of Rin-Tin-Tin but releases him and steps aside after realizing how deeply he loves Rose.

Author Max Wilk recalled visiting the set of *Tiger Rose* when he was a child. He remembered, "Miss Velez was a beautiful, busty young lady, who seemed to be enjoying herself, and kept on very good terms with the cast and crew."

Tiger Rose premiered in New York on Christmas Eve of 1929 as the inaugural film of the Beacon Theater before a capacity crowd of more than 3,000. *The New York Times* spent almost as much space describing the new cinema palace as the movie itself—"an audible film with Lupe Velez and Monte Blue in the principal roles." (There was no mention of her performance other than that, despite the fact that she was the star!)

Lupe entered the 1930s as one of the most popular young actresses in Hollywood. Her first film of the new decade was *Hell Harbor,* directed by the veteran Henry King. Based on Rida Johnson Young's novel *Out of the Night,* it was photographed on location near Tampa, Florida. Lupe was joined Gibson Gowland and Jean Hersholt who had previously costarred in Erich von Stroheim's *Greed.* Often mentioned as one of the greatest films of all time, *Greed* was originally intended to be nine hours long but was butchered to a more acceptable two hour length by the studio. The final scene was filmed in 130 degree heat in Death Valley.

The heat was so intense that Jean Hersholt spent several months in the hospital recovering from the ordeal.

Hersholt, born in Copenhagen, was well-known for his charity work. He founded the Motion Picture Relief Fund and received two Academy Awards in recognition of his humanitarian efforts. In his honor, the Jean Hersholt Humanitarian Award is presented from time to time at the Academy Awards.

Rondo Hatton appeared in *Hell Habor* in the supporting role as the dance hall proprietor. Hatton suffered from acromegaly, a disease of the pituitary gland which causes enlargement of the face, hands, and feet. Grotesquely disfigured by the disease, Hatton was the only monster ever to appear without make-up. He played a series of stranglers and backbreakers; his most memorable role was as the "Creeper" in the Sherlock Holmes film, *The Pearl of Death*.

Hell Harbor, set in the Caribbean, is a tale of love, greed, and murder. Lupe plays Anita Morgan, the daughter of the owner of a trading post, Harry Morgan (Gibson Gowland), and the unscrupulous descendant of the notorious Morgan the Pirate. A middle-aged pearl trader named Joseph Horngold (Jean Hersholt) blackmails Morgan to allow him to marry Anita in return for his silence about a murder Morgan had committed. The strong-willed Anita, meanwhile, has set her cap for a handsome American, Bob Wade (John Holland). In the climax, Morgan kills Horngold by throwing a knife through the latter's heart. Lupe received positive reviews with *The New York Times*' Mordaunt Hall citing her performance as "vivacious and believable," although it called the film "stagnant drama."

Lupe was subject to wild mood swings but she was usually dependable on the set. Critic John Champan described her unpredictable behavior: "Her temperament is just an excess of enthusiasm; if she is happy she is wildly so; if she is sad she is sad as hell. She is a raucous horse-player and gagger around the set, buzzing around with the speed and lack of direction of a big horsefly; but once a director calls for action she is instantly quiet, onto her job, and respectful of her boss."

Lupe's next five films were made at Universal Studios. *The Storm* was directed by William Wyler. Born in Alsace-Lorraine, Wyler was to become the most honored director in Hollywood, receiving a record twelve Oscar nominations and winning three Academy Awards during his career. This version was a loose remake of the 1922 Laura La Plante silent.

Lupe played Manette Fanchand, an "ingenuous" (*The New York Times*) French Canadian whose smuggler father is fleeing from the Northwest Mounted Police. She and her father hole up in a snowbound mountain cabin with two men (William "Stage" Boyd and Paul Cavanaugh). They both fall in love with Manette and become bitter rivals for her attention. "Miss Velez here possesses a vivacity typical of the roles in which she has previously appeared," *The New York Times* wrote, "but it is somehow curbed by the restraint shown by the other players." An interesting footnote was that one of the rivals was played by the actor whose scandal nearly destroyed the career of namesake William Boyd of *Hopalong Cassidy* fame. Director William Wyler panned *The Storm*, calling it the worst movie he ever made.

During the filming of *The Storm*, Gary Cooper decided to visit Lupe on location in Truckee, California. Due to their separate film careers, they had not seen each other in several weeks and they decided to make up for lost time. Before they retired to Lupe's sleeping car, Cooper painted red lipstick all over the exposed portions of Lupe's skin. Their lovemaking was so violent that the sleeping car creaked.

Lupe next costarred with handsome Lew Ayres and fast-rising Edward G. Robinson in *East is West*. Jean Hersholt was originally cast as the Chinese chop suey king, Charlie Yong, but his Danish accent was so ludicrous and incongruous that the preview audience laughed him off the screen. Robinson, on the verge of screen stardom (*Little Caesar* was to be his next film), was paid $100,000 to reshoot his scenes.

Robinson was born Emmanuel Goldenberg in Bucharest, Romania. After he came to America he changed his name to Edward G. Robinson. When asked what the initial G. stood for he replied, "God only knows or gangster." Actually the middle initial stood for nothing.

Robinson originally wanted to be a rabbi. Ironically, the man who became famous playing gangsters, studied to be a lawyer and earned a Masters Degree from Columbia. He spoke nine languages and used his linguistic skills during World War II to make broadcasts to Europe. Over the years, Robinson amassed one of the greatest collections of modern art in the world. "You don't collect paintings, they collect you," he said.

Only 5'5", Robinson described himself as "short, swarthy, and stocky." John Huston, who directed Robinson in Key Largo, said, "He looked like a crustacean without its shell."

In spite of his homely appearance, Robinson was a

charming and cultured man. Robinson's personal life
was troubled; his wife, Gladys, was a manic depressive.
Lupe did not try to conceal her attraction to Robinson,
an unlikely leading man, as he wrote in his autobiography, *All My Yesterdays:* "Sex was her game and she
played it on stage and off the stage. I could deal with
the rubbing and roving hands; off-stage I had my [mari-
tal] troubles. But I managed to elude her. Because she
was a hot tomato and I was not a rock, it was not easy."

The same year he made *East is West*, Robinson created a sensation with his performance in *Little Caesar*.
His portrayal of Rico Randello became the prototype
for gangsters in films but he never felt comfortable
playing hoodlums. When he fired a machine gun, Robinson always closed his eyes, forcing the director to
tape them open.

Lupe's other costar in the film, Lew Ayres, was discovered playing a banjo in Ray West's Orchestra at the
Cocoanut Grove by Paul Bern (later to find himself in
film lore as the man who married blonde bombshell
Jean Harlow and caused a scandal when he committed
suicide shortly after their wedding). In 1930, Ayres
starred in the acclaimed antiwar film, *All Quiet on the
Western Front*. His sensitive performance as a war-
weary soldier made him a star overnight.

A decade later his real life antiwar stance nearly
ruined his career. In the late 1930s, Ayres created the
Dr. Kildare character whom he portrayed in several
successful films. At the outbreak of World War II,
Ayres declared himself as a conscientious objector. He
was not prepared for the adverse reaction which followed. During the war, however, Ayres risked his life in
France as an ambulance driver, medic, and a chaplain's

aide but the public never understood his opposition to combat.

East Is West opens in China where Ming Toy (Lupe Velez) is put on the auction block. American Billy Benson (Lew Ayres) saves her from being sold to white slavers and sends her to San Francisco to begin a new life. Her spirited behavior gets her into trouble with the waterfront missionary society and she is sold to half-caste Charlie Yong (Edward G. Robinson), the local chop suey king. Once again Billy Benson arrives just in time to save her from Yong's clutches. Billy wants to wed Ming Toy but his patrician parents object to him marrying a foreigner. Their happiness is secured when they learn that Lupe is really the daughter of American missionaries, murdered when she was a baby.

"The story is trashy fiction of the sort that the paper pulp magazines publish only with reluctance at this late day," *The New York Times* found, but noted that "Lupe Velez makes the most of her role as Ming Toy." *East Is West* was the favorite movie of Robinson's close friends, George Burns and Gracie Allen. Burns and Allen did a hilarious take-off of Robinson and Lupe Velez.

Lupe repeated her role of Ming Toy in the Spanish-language version of *East Is West* entitled *Oriente Es Occidente*, with Barry Norton in the Lew Ayres role. Her popularity outside of the United States was at its peak. South of the border, she maintained her reputation as a serious actress, rather than as just a movie star.

Her next film, *Resurrection*, based on a novel by Leo Tolstoy, was directed by Edwin Carewe, who had discovered Lupe's longtime rival, Dolores Del Rio, at a tea party in Mexico and eventually married her. (Del Rio in fact had starred in the 1927 version). Fiery Lupe had surpassed the classically beautiful Del Rio as a box-office attraction. Playing opposite Lupe in *Resurrection* was the handsome, mustached John Boles who specialized in high-bred roles. He plays Prince Dimitri Nekhludoff who seduces the peasant girl, Katerina Maslova (Lupe Velez). She gives birth to his child but the infant dies. After being abandoned by the prince she sinks into a life of prostitution, indirectly causes the death of a merchant, and faces being sent to Siberia. Dimitri returns to profess his love for her but she accepts her sentence and goes into exile.

The New York Times' Mordaunt Hall felt that Lupe Velez's "performance is the chief asset of the production [although] even with the painstaking acting of Miss Velez most of the glimpses seem very far from Russia. Added to this the dialogue is amateurishly written." Lupe also made a Spanish language version of the film, co-starring Gilbert Roland, who over the years was one of Lupe's favorite dates.

Born Luis Antonio Damaso de Alonso in Mexico he chose the screen name Gilbert Roland in honor of his two favorite actors, John Gilbert and Ruta Roland. The studio had suggested the name John Adams but since it had already been taken by the second President of the United States, he rejected it. Roland began in films as a stand-in for Ramon Novarro. He was tall, dark, and extremely handsome, with black hair and green eyes. In 1925, he played opposite Clara Bow in *The Plastic Age*. They became lovers and were engaged to be married. Roland was devastated when Bow left him for director Victor Fleming. He challenged Fleming to a duel which fortunately was never fought.

Roland, who remained close to Lupe throughout her life, was a leading man until the mid-1930s when Fox stopped making Spanish-language films. Reduced to supporting roles, he appeared in several Cisco Kid features in the 1940s and continued acting on the screen for the next four decades.

While Gilbert Roland was a frequent companion, there still remained only one man in Lupe's life—Gary Cooper.

8

Alice Cooper

Gary Cooper was asked what was the most exciting thing that had ever happened to him in Hollywood. He replied without hesitation, "Lupe Velez!"

After a magazine ran a story that Cooper was interested in falconry, a fan in Montana sent him two golden eagles. Since Lupe loved birds he assumed she wouldn't mind keeping them at her Laurel Canyon retreat. When he arrived at her door carrying a huge cage, Lupe exploded in a rage.

"What have you got there, Gary?" she asked.

"Eagles. They won't give you a bit of trouble."

"What do you think you're going to do with those monsters?"

"Keep them in your backyard."

"Are you crazy?" she screamed.

Cooper eventually persuaded her to keep the eagles and built a huge cage for them in her backyard. Lupe complained that he paid more attention to the birds than he did to her. He called them lovebirds but she always referred to them as vultures. When the news-papers learned about the gift they ran a headline, "Gary Gives Lupe the Bird." In return, Lupe gave Gary pets which more reflected her personality—two wildcats.

Lupe bred prize-winning chihuahuas which com-peted in the Beverly Hills Charity Dog Show. She had a specially-made basket installed on her bicycle so she could take her favorite dogs, Mr. Kelly and Mrs. Mur-phy, along with her. It was a common sight to see Lupe pedaling around Hollywood with her dogs propped up on the handlebars. She also owned seventy-five ca-naries and knew every one of them by name.

Rumors were circulating that Lupe Velez and Gary Cooper were going to get married. Hedda Hopper wrote: "There was a spark between Lupe and Gary. We all thought they might elope eventually, regardless of the consequences." Lupe did everything she could to promote the marriage. "Of course I love him. Marry him? Well, who will know what I do until I do it. Maybe, tomorrow. Maybe, never. But I think, maybe."

Cooper was noncommittal on the subject. He be-lieved that it was unwise for a young leading man to marry because it would damage his reputation as a matinee idol. He said, "I am going to marry, someday. I want, like almost any man, a home and a family. I want a permanent union, not one of those impermances."

The biggest stumbling block to a wedding was his mother, Alice Cooper. When introduced to Lupe, Alice was appalled. Gary described his parents' reac-tion to Lupe this way:

"My folks didn't know what to make of her. Her

exuberant Latin spirits baffled mother, but Dad was
charmed into helpless laughter. If she started tearing
our house apart with one of her extravagant dances,
dad would put on one of his judge-of-the-supreme
court look, but that would only inspire her to more
outrageous goings-on. When she was exhausted she
would climb into his lap, grab his ear, and say, 'You do
love me, Judge, don't you? You love Lupe make
whoopee.' "

Judge Cooper tried to reassure his wife that the relationship wouldn't last. He reminded her that even the
prize bulls on their Montana ranch sometimes strayed.

Although he was nearly thirty, Gary was still a
mama's boy and Alice Cooper maintained a powerful
influence on her son. She was a proper Englishwoman
with an intimidating countenance. Actress Esther
Ralston said, "She looked like Queen Mary." In private
Alice did everything she could to undermine Gary's
relationship with Lupe. She referred to Lupe as "that
Mexican thing" and implied that she wasn't good
enough for her son. Without justification, she told
Gary that Lupe was cheating on him. She feigned
illnesses and when that didn't work, she threatened to
kill herself if he married Lupe.

Alice Cooper tried to rekindle his interest in Evelyn
Brent, a cultured actress with whom he had been involved prior to meeting Lupe. Brent seemed to be the
only one of Gary's many loves of whom Alice Cooper
approved. She said, "Evelyn Brent has been good to
Gary; she has given him poise, she has taught him to
think, her influence has been excellent, and I will always regard her with affection and gratitude."

Evelyn Brent made her reputation playing screen vamps and gangsters' molls. Her smoldering eyes, as they were described, gave her a sultry presence and her dark-haired beauty made her a favorite of the studio's glamour photographers. During *Don Juan* with John Barrymore, she set a screen record with 191 kisses (almost a kiss every thirty seconds) and her scenes of sexual passion in Howard Hughes' production of *The Mating Call* were considered steamy in her day. Before he met Marlene Dietrich, director Josef von Sternberg used Brent as his femme fatale in silent classics such as *The Last Command, Underworld,* and *The Dragnet.*

Brent's portrayal of gun moll Feathers McCoy in *Underworld* made her a star. Feathers' motto was: "You have to be bad to be good." *Underworld,* with its swift action and shocking violence, set the standard for the Hollywood gangsters films which would follow. Brent's portrayal was so convincing that actual gangsters praised her performance and she was dubbed "Queen of the Underworld."

She met Gary Cooper when they did *Beau Sabreur* in 1928. Years later Brent reflected on their relationship, "It was quite a thing, but it didn't last long. The women were so crazy about him. More than any other man I knew. I think what attracted people was he had a great shyness. He kept pulling back, and it intrigued people."

By her own admission she wasn't much of a party girl. When *Underworld* premiered she was afraid to go to the theater alone and asked Gary Cooper to accompany her. At the time she was a much bigger star than Cooper and he was embarrassed because he didn't know how to act at the premiere.

Cooper admired Brent and respected her intelligence but she was a little too tame for his taste. He told *Photoplay* in 1929: "In Evelyn Brent I found the companionship of a woman who was wise and brilliant. I was first attracted to her as a woman who had her feet on the ground and was not riding the rails."

Unlike Alice Cooper, Evelyn Brent expressed her admiration of Velez. "Now you take Lupe," she told writer John Kobal. "She should have been a bigger star than she was, but she frittered too much time away. She was off on a tangent all the time, she was excitable . . . she had a great talent, she had a great excitement about her. Lupe Velez had a vibrant something."

Brent spoiled Alice Cooper's plan when she unexpectedly married director Harry Edwards. Her career nosedived when talking pictures were introduced. Her posing, which was so effective in silent films, did not translate well into talkies. Actress Louise Brooks, who appeared in two films with Brent, described her technique: "Evelyn's idea of acting was to march into a scene, spread her legs and stand flat-footed and read her lines with masculine defiance." Brooks found her warm and friendly on the exterior but slyly observed, "But I found later she was like Baked Alaska — very cold inside."

Evelyn Brent's career rapidly declined. In 1928, after the success of *Underworld*, she appeared in seven films; by 1934 she made none. Unlike many stars who chose to retire rather than accept bit roles, Evelyn Brent found her name steadily sliding down the cast list, all but forgotten.

In desperation, Lupe Velez decided to make her feud with Alice Cooper public. She told a reporter, "I hope she never cries the tears I have cried. I hope she never knows the suffering I have known. I didn't hate her that much. She said I wasn't good enough for Gary. She told him I wasn't faithful to him. He believed what she told him."

Lupe began to blame Gary for his mother's interference. "Gary, it's all your fault when your mama spits when she sees me."

Lupe and Alice Cooper said more to each other in print than they did in person. Alice Cooper defended herself in a fan magazine article entitled, "Gary's Mother Speaks at Last."

"I have no ill feelings toward Lupe Velez. I wish her continued success. I think she is a fine little actress. I wish her happiness. My only regret is that she finds it necessary to talk so openly and so violently for publication. Her love for Gary, I should think, would make her want to keep it a secret thing, rather than allow it to be public property. . . . It shocks me, of course, to read headlines that I have invaded Lupe's home . . . to get personal nicknacks that belong to Gary. And to hear the stories, no matter how grossly exaggerated they may be, that she demands of Gary that I be kept from bothering her. I haven't seen Lupe in months.

"And preposterous stories that I threatened to kill myself if Gary married Lupe, and that if he did, I said it would break my heart. And that I made a long trip to New York. . . . to tell him that his sweetheart was unfaithful to him. Do mothers do that? Certainly I don't. And the stories that I had told friends that Lupe wasn't good enough to marry my boy.

"I had never set down any dictates about the kind of girl my son should marry. I rely too much on his innate good taste, his judgment, his intelligence. He knows whom he wants to marry, and he will marry her when the time comes. It will not be the duty of his father nor myself to select his wife for him. . . .

"Perhaps I have not entirely approved of the women with whom Gary has been romantically associated. But does any mother entirely approve of her son's choice? Very seldom. . . . There are qualities, of course, that I should like to see in Gary's wife. The most important are respectability and fairmindedness. I leave the matter of beauty and talent and charm up to him. I don't care whether she is blonde or brunette, or whether or not she is an actress. After all, why should I?"

Mrs. Cooper needn't have worried because other factors were about to tear Gary and Lupe apart. In 1930, Gary Cooper costarred with the exotic and glamorous Marlene Dietrich in Josef von Sternberg's *Morocco,* and quietly became involved in an affair which was one of Hollywood's worst kept secrets.

Dietrich was born Maria Magdalene Von Losch, the daughter of a German army officer killed on the Russian front in 1915. She sold gloves to make a living but her real ambition was to become a concert violinist. Her career as a violinist came to an end when she pulled a ligament in her middle finger while playing a Bach sonata. She was reduced to playing accompaniment for silent films; it appeared to be as close as she would ever get to being in the movies. She married a chicken farmer and settled down for an apparent life of domesticity.

That all changed when she was discovered by famed producer Max Reinhardt. She was invited to a party at Reinhardt's castle and entertained guests by playing a musical saw. When Dietrich played she spread and revealed her gorgeous legs. Noticeably aroused, Reinhardt gave Dietrich her start in films.

For years her career sputtered. In 1929, it appeared that she was on her way to stardom when director G. W. Pabst picked her to play Lulu in *Pandora's Box*. Just as Dietrich was about to sign the contract, Pabst changed his mind and selected American actress Louise Brooks. The role brought film immortality to Brooks and left Dietrich devastated.

Her disappointment was short-lived. That same year she was chosen by director Josef von Sternberg to play the part of cabaret singer Lola Lola in *The Blue Angel*. Dietrich was not the first choice for the role. Brigitte Helm, the star of *Metropolis*, was the first choice but bowed out when she had an emergency appendectomy. Phyllis Haver was the next choice but she decided to retire from acting after she married a millionaire.

Von Sternberg immediately went to work to transform the plump German actress into a film goddess. He adjusted her hairline and made her lose 30 pounds. He had a dentist remove her back teeth to give her the sunken cheek look which became one of her trademarks. Another change was to have her eyebrows plucked and pencilled in higher on her forehead. Von Sternberg even went so far as to have Dietrich's ankles massaged free of fat. Once the transformation was complete, her androgynous allure made her a serious rival to Garbo.

Dietrich soon adapted a lifestyle worthy of a movie star. For instance, the chauffeur of her Cadillac limousine wore a mink-trimmed uniform and carried a

matching set of revolvers. Dietrich was confident that
she had lured Gary Cooper away from the sexpot from
south of the border, "He was finally rid of Lupe Velez,
who had been at his heels throughout the making of
Morocco," she said.

Lupe was determined to keep her man at all costs,
and she retaliated by doing an outrageous impersonation of Dietrich at parties, much to the embarrassment
of Gary Cooper. After the filming of *Morocco* ended,
Cooper's affair with Dietrich cooled (it would be re-
kindled years later when they worked together in *Desire*) and he returned to Lupe Velez.

A more unexpected rival for Cooper's attention was
Anderson Lawler. A handsome young actor with wavy
blond hair, Lawler had came to Hollywood from Broadway. He became good friends with Cooper and often
tagged along on his dates with Lupe. At first Lupe
didn't mind his presence. "He was a good referee for
our fights," she said.

Lupe's enthusiasm for Anderson Lawler soon waned.
He was everything she was not; sophisticated, articu-
late, and witty. He shared many of Gary Cooper's
outdoor interests such as swimming, hunting, and
horseback riding. Lawler was knowledgeable on the
subjects of music, art, and literature. Cooper and Lawler attended plays and concerts together and soon
Lupe felt she was the one who was tagging along.

Lupe was shocked when Cooper moved in with Lawler, particularly when it became known that Lawler was
a homosexual. It was obvious to everyone that Lawler
was in love with Cooper. Lupe decided she would try
to find out if the rumors about the two men being
lovers were true. In public, she unzipped Gary Coo-

per's fly to see if she could smell any traces of Anderson Lawler's cologne. The experiment was inconclusive.

As Lupe's jealousy increased, her behavior became more unstable. On one occasion she and Gary were invited to a party at Marion Davies' fabulous beach house on the Pacific Coast Highway in Santa Monica, a $7 million bungalow known as Ocean Front. It was the largest beachfront house in California with thirty bedrooms and fifteen bathrooms. The swimming pool was so vast that a Venetian marble bridge was constructed to span it. Ocean Front was so enormous that it was later converted into a hotel.

The interior was even more ornate. The Marine Room, where games were played, was paneled in English walnut, and the Music Room contained ceiling murals and a breathtaking ocean view. Priceless paintings by the old masters hung on the walls of the dining room which featured a room-long dining table, oriental rugs, and a crystal chandelier. Undoubtedly, the Gold Room was the most spectacular one in the house. It seemed to be touched by Midas; everything in it was covered with gold. The walls were decorated in gold leaf, the draperies were covered with gold brocade, and the chairs were upholstered in gold.

The hostess, Marion Davies, was an actress more renowned for her thirty-year affair with publisher William Randolph Hearst than for her screen credits. Hearst had spotted the blonde beauty in the chorus of the *Ziegfeld Follies* when she was nineteen. For eight weeks he attended every performance, buying two tickets, one for himself and the other for his hat. Despite being married and thirty-five years older than Davies, Hearst made her his mistress.

Hearst set out to make Marion Davies the biggest star in Hollywood. He ordered his newspapers to mention her name at least once every day. He created the Cosmopolitan Production Company just to produce her films. Her dressing room was stuffed with antiques and staffed with servants. Despite Hearst's best efforts, Marion Davies' film career was only a modest success. Actually she was a gifted comedienne and the publicity overkill probably damaged her career.

Marion Davies, who had a distracting stutter, was a gracious and popular hostess at both Ocean Front and Hearst's palatial retreat, San Simeon. She loved ice cream and was once challenged by Howard Hughes to an ice cream eating contest which she won easily. The only thing she loved more than ice cream was parties. She loved to throw extravagant costume soirees with various themes. One year it would be an Early American party, the next would have a covered wagon theme.

Lupe loved to be the center of attention at parties and liked to make a scene. Designer Travis Banton remembered, "She would burst into a room, happy and carefree. She would think nothing of attending the coronation of a king in blazing red and yellow pajamas with three feathers stuck on the top of her head."

During one of Davies' parties Lupe complained to the guests that Gary Cooper had tried to sexually assault her. Considering that they had been involved in a well-publicized affair for more than two years, Lupe's cries of attempted rape were ignored.

Lupe believed that occasional violence should be part of any healthy relationship. According to her, there were only two important things in life — love and fighting. She said, "The way to a happy marriage is to fight once a week, maybe more."

Even the most romantic moment could suddenly erupt into violence. Once, Gary Cooper was sleeping peacefully at poolside. Lupe, kneeling beside him, asked, "Is he not beautiful? I have never seen anyone so beautiful as my Gary."

Cooper was only pretending to be asleep and heard everything she said. He snickered at her compliments which enraged Lupe.

"You laugh at Lupe's love?"

She furiously attacked Cooper and began punching and scratching him. It took every bit of his strength to subdue her. Lupe was aroused by the violence and the fights were often followed by intense lovemaking.

Lupe always loved boxing and attended the fights every Friday at the Hollywood Legion Stadium. Her histrionics at the bouts became part of Hollywood lore. Adela Rogers St. Johns wrote of the experience: "Hollywood to this moment has no more vivid memories than that of Lupe Velez at the Hollywood Legion fights. Visiting celebrities were always taken there, not to see the bouts, but to see Lupe rooting, putting on a better show than the one in the ring."

As soon as the opening bell rang, Lupe was down at ringside, yelling encouragement to her favorite fighters, usually Latins. When the action wasn't going her way, she would curse and pound on the ring apron. Sometimes, if she did not agree with the decision, she would jump into the ring and assault the referee. Once in the ring she liked to whirl and pull her dress over her head which was made all the more exciting by the fact that she didn't wear underpants. Her favorite boxer

With E. Alyn Warren, Lew Ayres and Edward G. Robinson in
East Is West (1930).

With Warner Baxter in De Mille's *The Squaw Man* (1931).

In the arms of Monte Blue in *Tiger Rose* (1929).

As the Wild Mountain Girl, in a passionate dance scene with Douglas Fairbanks in *The Gaucho* (1927).

Dressed to attend the opera, with Rod La Rocque in *Stand and Deliver* (1928).

Flirting with William Boyd in D.W. Griffith's *Lady of the Pavements* (1929), as William Blakewell and Albert Conti watch.

With Lon Chaney in *Where East Is East* (1929).

An autographed glamour photo from the 1930s.

With Metropolitan Opera star Lawrence Tibbett
in *Cuban Love Song* (1931).

Randolph Scott, the man in Lupe's life after her
breakup with John Gilbert.

With Melvyn Douglas in *The Broken Wing* (1932).

With wheelchair-bound Walter Huston in *Kongo* (1932).

With Frank Morgan in *The Half Naked Truth* (1932).

At odds with Lee Tracy in *The Half Naked Truth* (1932).

was named Bert Colima. Whenever he fought she
would scream throughout the bout, "Give it to him!" If
he lost, she would cry uncontrollably.

Sometimes her presence actually affected the outcome of a fight as writer Budd Schulberg recalled:

"How many times had we seen the tempestuous
Lupe in the front row at the Hollywood Legion Stadium, pounding on the blood-stained canvas of the ring
and screaming profane Mexican incantations at brown-
skinned countrymen who were failing to living up to
her high standards of combat? One night we had seen
her stand up and cup her hands to shout some words of
pugilistic wisdom to a light, handsome Mexican-Indian
lightweight named Rojas. Rojas turned to look at Lupe.
Lupe was easy to look at. In fact he had been openly
flirting with her between rounds. Even I, who pro-
fessed to hate girls, and who was surrounded by young
women whose profession it was to be pretty, often
found myself staring at Lupe. So Rojas turned his head
and looked down the better to hear Lupe's advice. It
was the last thing he heard for several minutes as he lay
unconscious on the canvas, his head so close to Lupe's
that she could have reached out and cradled her fallen
gladiator in her arms. Instead she was screaming, 'Hijo!
Get up, you son-of-a-bitch . . .'

"Another time I was at the Friday-night Hollywood
Legion fights with my father in one of his prized regular seats in the first press row, when a tall, skinny-
legged Mexican fighter, whose name I remember only
as Tony, started to bleed from the corner of his left eye.
Blood kept running down his eye, blinding his vision
and smearing his face. At the end of each round the
referee would go over to examine the injury. Tony's

handlers would protest that the wound was not serious, and the fight was allowed to continue. Now the eye was a bloody mess, an angry pool of blood that no longer resembled an eye. Father and other first-row fans held their programs up against their faces to protect them from the spray of blood. I heard the screaming, I saw our Mexican sexpot, hysteric Lupe Velez, pounding on the apron of the ring to urge on her blinded compatriot, watched the terrible wound in his face grow larger and larger, and suddenly I felt as if I was inside that eye and this time I saw red circles spinning, spinning, spinning . . ."

Lupe was emotionally unpredictable and would suddenly burst into laughter or tears for no apparent reason. She would attack Gary Cooper without provocation. His passivity enraged her even more. She meant it when she said, "I think I will kill my Gary because he does not get angry when Lupe is angry with him."

Apparently only once did Gary Cooper ever strike her. One day he reported to the studio with scratch marks all over his face. He admitted to a friend, "I'm a little black-and-blue, but I let her have it."

"You mean you hit her?" his friend asked in disbelief.

"No, kind of slapped her."

"So it's all over between you two?"

"Nope, happens all the time."

Cooper always regretted hitting her, even in self defense. He explained what had caused the accident: "She was the only one I could fully trust, but I thought she was running around and said so. She threw the first punch. I was just trying to calm her down."

Cooper was beginning to realize that Lupe Velez was out of control and becoming dangerous. She kept a loaded pistol in her dresser and carried a razor sharp stiletto in her garter. Lupe claimed she carried the knife for protection. Gary, it turned out, was the one who needed the protection.

Frequently she lunged at Cooper with the knife when she was angry but he was usually able to fend her off. The exception occurred one night when Cooper was busy cooking. Out of nowhere, Lupe rushed at him with the knife and stabbed him in the arm. She bragged for years that she was the only woman to leave her mark on Gary Cooper.

Lupe hinted that Cooper had his own violent streak: "Coop has a temper which no one knows about. He belted [Carole] Lombard and he belted Clara [Bow]. And he belted me good . . . I'm Lupe! I tell you what I think is truth. Real problem that Cooper has. He runs for women who are not like his mama! So sweet, eh? And always he is right and perfect. He gets excited when we fight, and I tell you one thing. Lupe was the only one who scarred him for life. I got him with a knife once . . . in the arm, and he sweat and bled. Boy, he sweat. We were cooking dinner and Gary could not duck this time. He has the scars. . . . The press calls me wild. Ha! They do not know the real Cooper. They will never know the real cowboy. Never! I know him and love him."

Cooper's constant battles with Lupe left him drained depressed and he turned to drink. He would show up unannounced at actress Myrna Loy's house. Loy had just arrived in Hollywood and still lived with her mother. Cooper would be disconsolate and Loy would calm him as if he were a child. One afternoon, she discovered Cooper slumped in a chair on her porch, staring blankly into space. She recalled, "He looked so forlorn and vulnerable, utterly touching, with that long body sort of crumpled, those fine eyes clouded."

When Loy walked over to him Cooper, in a daze, called out, "Mother?"

The sometimes violent relationship with Lupe was finally taking its toll on Gary Cooper. Lupe's attacks were becoming more frequent and Cooper feared for his life. He suffered a nervous breakdown. His doctor described his condition as a complete physical collapse. Cooper had lost 40 pounds and suffered from jaundice. His doctors informed him that he would need at least a year of complete rest to fully recover. Cooper realized that the only way he would recover was to get away from Lupe.

The studio agreed to grant him a six month leave of absence to recuperate. Cooper secretly planned an European vacation. He went incognito to the railroad station to catch the Twentieth Century to Chicago, unaware that he was being stalked. Lupe Velez had somehow learned of his departure, and decided that if she couldn't have him then no woman would.

Just as he was about to board the train, Lupe yelled, "Gary, you son-of-a-bitch!" She pulled out her revolver and fired. The bullet narrowly missed Cooper's head and he dove into the train. Lupe cursed her bad marksmanship as she hurried away before she could be apprehended.

9

The Countess Di Frasso

Gary Cooper's publicist released a statement that the couple had "drifted apart." Lupe blamed Alice Cooper for the breakup. "He may be an idol to his mother, but he's less than nothing to me. I don't love Gary Cooper. I don't love anybody. I will never marry. I stay Lupe. I am sick of love."

She couldn't understand why Cooper had left her. "I tried to make him happy. I did make him happy. I would have done anything in the world for him."

Meanwhile, Gary Cooper had already become involved with another woman. Traveling to Italy, hoping to regain his health, he was introduced by producer Walter Wanger to a friend, the Countess di Frasso, in Rome.

The Countess di Frasso was born Dorothy Taylor, the daughter of Bertrand Taylor, a New York leather goods manufacturer who had amassed a fortune of over $50 million. Dorothy's grandfather had been the governor of New York and her brother was the president of the New York Stock Exchange.

She had inherited more than $12 million and had wed aviator Claude Graham, who had an airplane painted on their bedroom ceiling. The marriage ended when she caught him sleeping with her best friend.

Her next marriage was to an Italian count nearly thirty years her senior. In spite of his title, the Count di Frasso was penniless at the time of the wedding. Their marriage was one of convenience; she wanted his title and he needed her money. They lived at the Villa Madama, a palatial residence whose walls were adorned with paintings by Raphael and ceiling showcased a magnificent fresco by Leonardo da Vinci. Incredibly, the villa was being used as a cow barn and the Countess spent a million dollars to restore it to its former glory. The Villa Madama became the gathering place for the international elite. The Duke of York, who later became King George VI of England, was a frequent guest.

The Countess had never heard of Gary Cooper when he arrived. Her friend, Elsa Maxwell, had told her that Cooper was "short, fat, and plain." The Countess took one took at the tall, handsome actor, turned to Maxwell and said, "I might have known you would have your joke."

She was instantly attracted to Cooper, who was in terrible shape, suffering from exhaustion and jaundice. Without prompt medical treatment there was fear for his life. The Countess immediately sent him to bed and provided around-the-clock treatment from the finest physicians in Rome. Once she nursed him back to health, the Countess seduced Cooper. The Count was a willing cuckold, considering Cooper to be his friend and encouraging him to stay at the Villa Madama as long as he wished.

At forty-three, the Countess di Frasso was thirteen years older than Cooper, but still a very attractive woman. Buxom, with frosty blue eyes and black hair, she was a dynamic, cultured woman with a racy wit. The Countess di Frasso dressed in elegant gowns and wore expensive jewelry. Above all, she possessed a strong will which demanded that she always got what she wanted. And she wanted Gary Cooper.

The Countess was determined to make a continental gentleman out of the American cowboy. She took him to the finest tailor in Rome and bought him a complete new wardrobe. Before he met the Countess, Cooper wore checkered suits, loud ties, and gaudy clothes. Mrs. Jack Warner, wife of the studio boss, commented on the sartorial metamorphosis, "He went to Rome looking like a cowboy and he came back looking like a prince." The Countess was the first to admit her influence, "I taught him everything he knows. When I met him, he was still wet behind the ears."

For the first time money became important to Gary Cooper. He appreciated the fine things money could buy and vowed that when he did marry it would be to a wealthy woman.

The Countess' next step was to introduce Cooper to European society. She threw parties in his honor and invited all the right people. Cooper remembered, "It was hard to tell whether the Countess threw one party that lasted all summer or a series of weekend parties that lasted all week. Guests just came and went as if the Villa Madama were a grand hotel. . . . Her villa was

the meeting place for the international set, and rubbing elbows with assorted noblemen, heiresses, and
celebrated characters made me forget my fears."

Cooper was renowned for his expert horsemanship
and the Countess arranged for him to ride with the
Italian cavalry. The cavalry officer, wanting to chal-
lenge Cooper's skill, chose the treacherous Tor Di
Quinto steeplechase course, considered the toughest
in Italy. Cooper surprised everybody by being one of
only four riders to complete the course.

When Paramount Studios learned of Cooper's strenuous activities, he was ordered home. As an entice-
ment, they raised his weekly salary from $1,000 to
$1,750. The Countess begged him to remain in Italy
and even made inquiries about buying the studio. Cooper feared that if he stayed, Paramount would termi-
nate his contract and he would become a kept man. He
had expected to spend a week in Rome and he stayed
ten.

The news of the romance had traveled quickly. Tallulah Bankhead displayed her acerbic wit when she
speculated that Cooper was probably "worn to a
frasso." Humorist Robert Benchley reportedly said, "I
always wanted to go to Europe on the Countess di
Frasso." Claire Booth Luce later wrote a play entitled
The Women, whose main characters, the Countess de
Lage and a cowboy named Buck Winston, were thinly
veiled portrayals of the Countess di Frasso and Gary
Cooper.

Gary Cooper returned to America in August 1931.
He downplayed his relationship with the Countess,
telling the press, "She and her husband were very
pleasant and hospitable when I was in Rome." Under-

standably, Cooper was nervous about how he was going to be received by Lupe Velez. After all, the last time he had seen her she had tried to shoot him. When they met Lupe asked Gary, "How's your grandmother?" referring to the Countess di Frasso.

Lupe continued to try to give the impression that she was the one who had dumped Cooper. She displayed bogus telegrams from Cooper asking for one more chance. She told reporters, "When Gary and I were in love it was terrible. I hate young men. They are so conceited . . . I got tired of Gary. I don't love Gary Cooper. I turned Cooper down because his parents didn't want me to marry him, and the studio thought it would injure his career. Now, it's over. I'm glad. I feel so free. I must be free. I know men too well. They are all the same, no? They fall in love with Lupe very much, the way Lupe is. Then quick, they want I should be somebody else — the doormat. They wish to conquer the fiery one, to tame Lupe. I die first."

Back in Italy, the lovesick Countess was about to launch a plan to lasso her cowboy. She contacted a friend in New York, a wealthy horse breeder named Jerome Preston, and instructed him to invite Cooper on a safari to Tanganyika. Cooper at first turned him down, but found the lure of adventure too great and accepted the invitation.

Arriving in Africa he was startled to find the Countess waiting for him. She had brought along many of her society friends but the Count was conspicuously absent. As she hoped, the romance was renewed. She lovingly recalled watching him by the campfire, "Coop was sitting away from the rest of us, silhouetted against the sky. It was the most beautiful picture I'd ever seen."

Gary Cooper proved to be an expert big game hunter, bagging over eighty animals during the five month safari. Cooper stayed at Preston's ranch on the shore of Lake Nyasa. He loved Africa so much that he seriously considered buying a ranch and moving there.

The Countess suggested that the entourage return to the Riviera. "Spring has come to the Riviera," she said. "What we need is a little caravan to tour the Mediterranean coast and visit a few of the watering places."

Paramount was not pleased by Cooper's extended absence and threatened to replace him with a young actor named Cary Grant. Cooper took note that Grant's first name sounded like his and that his initials were transposed. He was in Monte Carlo when the money finally ran out. The studio made one last attempt to lure Cooper back to Hollywood by offering him another $750 a week raise. The timing was perfect and Cooper wired Paramount that he was returning.

Because he was broke, the Countess paid for his transportation home. Cooper came back to Hollywood with the trophies from his safari. He also came back with the Countess di Frasso, although he had not requested her company. She had let him escape her grasp once and wasn't about to let it happen again. She bought a mansion on Chevy Chase Drive in Beverly Hills, conveniently only a few doors down from where Gary Cooper lived. The Countess immediately set up her salon and the international set invaded Hollywood. She even tried her hand at moviemaking when she unsuccessfully tried to sell her home movies of the safari to a studio.

Cooper denied being romantically involved with anyone, claiming he "was out of love temporarily." Fan magazines still tried to link him with Lupe Velez. One story had him sitting alone in Greta Garbo's old home (which he was renting) lamenting the loss of Lupe.

Lupe insisted she no longer lamented the loss of Gary. She hinted to the press that she had a mystery lover. "I am ever so much in love again. Who is he? I'll never tell. Nobody is going to know this time because that spoils everything when the public knows."

The mystery lover turned out to be John Gilbert. Gilbert had rivaled Valentino as the silent screen's greatest romantic idol. He believed his own press clippings and could never live up to his image as the great lover. His offscreen romance with Greta Garbo made headlines throughout the twenties. Gilbert's career went on the decline with the advent of the talkies. He had a pleasant tenor voice which sounded high-pitched and tinny on the screen. One explanation for his distorted voice may have been the primitive sound equipment being used. However, there may have been a more sinister reason.

Powerful M-G-M studio head Louis B. Mayer had a deep dislike for Gilbert, dating back to when he overheard Gilbert telling a story about his mother who had been a stage actress. Gilbert recalled an occasion when the train of her dress accidentally rolled up in the curtain during a performance. "That's the last time I saw my mother's ass," Gilbert joked. Mayer, who thought that disrespect for one's mother was the worst sin imaginable, was outraged, "That man's a monster! A degenerate!" he exclaimed.

Another time Gilbert joked that his mother was a whore. Mayer failed to see the humor and threatened, "I ought to cut his balls off." At the time Gilbert was the studio's most popular male star and Mayer temporarily put business considerations ahead of his personal feelings.

Gilbert's undoing may have been his love for Greta Garbo. Garbo had come to Hollywood from Sweden with her mentor, director Mauritz Stiller. Louis B. Mayer had sent for Stiller but the director insisted that his protege also be signed by the studio. Only a few years before, Garbo had been earning a dollar a week, lathering men's faces in a barbershop. Mayer took one look at Garbo and told her Americas didn't like fat women. It was suggested that she change her name to Gabor. When she arrived in New York in 1925, Garbo had to pay a photographer $10 to take her picture.

Irving Thalberg, the young production chief at M-G-M, also initially thought she was a hopeless case. He commented that she was flat-chested, had straight hips and bad teeth. At the studio's insistence, Garbo lost 20 pounds and had her teeth fixed. She was cast opposite John Gilbert in Flesh and the Devil and the chemistry between the two, both on and off the screen, was electrifying. Gilbert called Garbo "the most alluring creature I've ever seen." Suddenly, Greta Garbo was the hottest star in Hollywood.

John Gilbert became obsessed with Garbo and repeatedly asked her to marry him. Garbo, because of her solitary nature, opposed marriage and turned him down many times before finally accepting his proposal. The dream marriage of Hollywood's two biggest stars was scheduled to take place at Marion Davies' beach-house on September 8, 1926. At the last moment, Garbo changed her mind and literally left John Gilbert standing at the altar. In frustration and anger, Gilbert broke down and flung himself on the floor in a tantrum. Louis B. Mayer, seizing the opportunity, whispered in his ear, "Why don't you just fuck the dame and forget about marrying her?"

Gilbert grabbed Mayer and dragged him into the marble bathroom and attempted to strangle him. Surprisingly, the small, bespectacled Mayer had the reputation of being one of Hollywood's best fighters. He had once knocked out Charlie Chaplin with one punch after the comedian made a disparaging remark about his former wife, Mildred Harris. The same fate befell director Erich von Stroheim when he said, "All women are whores," during the filming of The Merry Widow. On this day, however, he was overpowered by the enraged Gilbert and might have been killed if his attacker hadn't been dragged off by members of the wedding party.

Mayer swore that John Gilbert was finished, even if it cost the studio a million dollars a year. The motto of M-G-M was: "More Stars Than There Are in Heaven." Mayer believed one less star wouldn't be missed. Gilbert's hatred of Mayer in return, was so great that he actually hired a bodyguard to keep him from killing his boss.

Mayer reportedly ordered his sound technicians to distort Gilbert's voice to make it sound effeminate. He made sure that Gilbert was cast in inferior movies. Mayer told one director of a Gilbert film, "You make that picture and you make it lousy!"

One of John Gilbert's first talkies was *His Glorious Night*. In the climactic scene, Gilbert confessed to his lover, "I love you. I love you. I love you." His high pitched voice brought squeals of laughter from the audience. The scene was brilliantly parodied a quarter of a century later in the M-G-M musical, *Singin' In The Rain*. Critics began to call Gilbert's films "shriekies."

The loss of Garbo and his own faltering career set John Gilbert on a self-destructive course. He began to drink heavily and secluded himself in his decaying mansion. His wife, actress Ina Claire, left him and delivered a fatal blow to his shattered ego when she told him she was a better actor than he was.

Gilbert hoped that Lupe Velez might be the antidote he needed to raise his spirits. Perhaps her zest for life might be contagious. Lupe promised to give it her best shot. "He hide in that big, gloomy house like a bear with a sore ear. His wife had told him she is a better actor than he is, which is true, but no wife should tell a man such things. I will make him laugh, that cure him."

When Gilbert continued to brood, Lupe tried a more direct approach. She scolded him. "Big baby, you let Hollywood get you down. I say Hollywood, look out, here comes Lupe. If my heart hurts me, I'll go to the fights and holler, 'Whoopee!' Hollywood says that Lupe, she is the Wild One, nothing ever gets her down."

For a time in 1931, John Gilbert and Lupe Velez were inseparable. One memorable Sunday afternoon, they attended a gathering at Norma Shearer and Irving Thalberg's beach house. Among the guests was the celebrated author, F. Scott Fitzgerald, the golden boy of American literature in the twenties whose writing career had recently sputtered as he took to the bottle.

Fitzgerald reluctantly came to Hollywood as a screenwriter for the Jean Harlow film, Red Headed Woman. His book royalties for the year was only $100 (the royalties for his masterpiece, *The Great Gatsby*, totaled $17). Fitzgerald wanted to make a good impression, particularly with Norma Shearer who was one of his favorite actresses, but he arrived at the party noticeably drunk.

Everybody at the party was expected to perform or entertain the other guests. When it came Fitzgerald's turn he asked Shearer if she would loan him her dog. He announced that he was going to sing and asked actor Ramon Novarro to accompany him on the piano. Holding the pet in his arms, Fitzgerald began to sing his drunken song to the dog.

The other guests tried to listen politely but the nonsensical song seemed to go on forever, and they reportedly stifled their laughter as Fitzgerald launched into verse after verse. By the fourth verse, Lupe Velez and John Gilbert began to hiss. Gradually, the guests left the room and only Norma Shearer, acting the part of the gracious hostess, remained.

The following day, Fitzgerald, in Hollywood at the time to pick up money writing screenplays, realized he had made a terrible mistake. He confided to a friend, "This job means a lot to me. I hope I didn't make too much of a jackass of myself." He needed the money desperately because his wife, Zelda, had suffered a breakdown and required constant care. The day after the party, Fitzgerald went to the M-G-M commissary to eat lunch. One of the films in production was a

horror movie, *Freaks*, which featured sideshow performers. Several of the freaks were eating lunch including the Hilton sisters, Siamese twins joined at the
spine. When Daisy Hilton asked her sister, Violet, what
she wanted for lunch, it was more than Fitzgerald
could take and he hurried from the room.

Fitzgerald was soon notified that he had been fired
by M-G-M. He had earned $5,826 for his stay in Holly-
wood, barely more than he could command for a short
story in his prime. He decided to write a short story
about his Hollywood experience. The result was
"Crazy Sunday," a thinly veiled account of his disas-
trous Sunday party at Norma Shearer's home. Even
though it was one of his best stories, he found it difficult to sell. Eventually, he sold it to a small publication,
American Mercury, for $200, a fraction of his nominal
fee. Years later, Fitzgerald returned to Hollywood
where he died of a heart attack in 1940 at the age of
forty-four, unappreciated by the studios and virtually
forgotten by the public.

In October 1931, John Gilbert embarked on a trip to
Europe. His contract provided for a three month vacation and he hoped to travel alone, at his own pace. He
hoped that a nice, quiet trip away from Hollywood
would restore his confidence.

Lupe Velez had already lost Gary Cooper as a result
of a European sojourn and was not going to let history
repeat itself with John Gilbert. She told Louella Parsons, "Yes, I love John Gilbert and I'm going to follow
him to Europe just as soon as I can get my passport.
Love was never like this."

Lupe joined Gilbert in Europe and never gave him a
moment's peace. He decided to cut short their vacation
and return home after only a month abroad. He discov-

ered that Lupe was not the ideal traveling companion. On their flight from Paris to Cherbourg, the weather was rough and Lupe became violently ill. They returned to America on the luxury liner *Mauretania,* but Lupe was constantly seasick and spent most of the voyage throwing up.

When they arrived in New York, Gilbert sent Lupe on to Hollywood, telling her he had to take care of some unfinished business. The unfinished business turned out to be his ex-wife, Ina Claire. When Lupe learned of her lover's infidelity—to her—she tried to make it appear that it was her idea for the split.

"You know I don't love Jack except I am his friend. All that I says to him, it restores his vanity. It is good for a man's vanity which is beat up to have it said that Lupe, the heartbreaker, she loves Gilbert, no?"

Ina Claire was less concerned about John Gilbert's fragile psyche. Known for her wicked sense of humor, she was asked by a reporter how it felt to be married to a celebrity. "Why don't you ask my husband?" she replied. She wanted no part of a reconciliation, further deflating Gilbert's ego.

John Gilbert slipped steadily into drink and depression. Once, at Marion Davies' beach house, Gilbert declared that he was going to commit suicide. Thinking he was kidding, some of the guests dared him to do it. "All right, I will," he said, as he walked toward the ocean. He walked into the waves but when the water got waist high he turned around and threw himself on the beach. He laid on the sand sobbing, "I can't do it."

His health and spirit broken, Gilbert suffered his first heart attack. Weak and pale, he was constantly attended by a male nurse during his recuperation. Marlene Dietrich came to his aid, nursing him back to health and getting him off the bottle. She became romantically involved with Gilbert and there was talk that they might get married. Then one day Greta Garbo showed up at Gilbert's house unexpectedly while Dietrich was there. He ran to her car, leaving Dietrich as though she wasn't even there. Gilbert begged Garbo to renew their relationship. He waited every day but she never returned.

Gilbert relapsed into heavy drinking. Dietrich was deeply hurt by the incident with her rival, Greta Garbo, but she could see that his health was failing rapidly and remained by his side. One afternoon they were playing tennis when John Gilbert had a seizure and collapsed on the court. Dietrich was horrified when handfuls of Gilbert's hair fell out.

In 1935, Marlene Dietrich was signed to star in a Frank Borzage film entitled *Desire*. The brilliant director Ernst Lubitsch was in charge of the production and Dietrich pleaded with him to cast John Gilbert in the leading role of the jewel thief. Lubitsch, aware of Gilbert's condition, reluctantly offered him the part. On the set it became apparent that Gilbert's health was worse than Lubitsch had expected. on January 9, 1936, Lubitsch replaced John Gilbert with Gary Cooper. He told Dietrich that he could not afford to risk the film on someone who might not live through the production.

The thought of being replaced by Marlene Dietrich's old lover, Gary Cooper, was more than John Gilbert could take. The next day he suffered a heart attack and was dead at the age of thirty-nine. At his funeral, a grief-stricken Marlene Dietrich collapsed in the aisle.

10

Cecil B. De Mille
and a Cast of Thousands

Lupe's volatile personal life had not yet affected her acting career. She was very much in demand as evidenced by director Cecil B. De Mille casting her as the Indian maiden, Naturich, in *The Squaw Man*. This was De Mille's third version of the film which launched his long career.

In 1913, Samuel Goldfish (who later changed his name to Goldwyn), a former glove salesman, and Jesse Lasky decided to go west to start their own film production company. In those days, New York was the center of the movie industry. However, since the setting for their first film, an Indian melodrama called *The Squaw Man*, was Arizona they decided to shoot on location in the west.

Their first choice for a director was D. W. Griffith but when he was unavailable they selected Cecil B. De Mille. De Mille originally wanted to film *The Squaw Man* in Flagstaff, Arizona, because it seldom rained there. However, when the crew arrived by train, Flagstaff was deluged with rain. It rained for a week and De Mille decided to look further west for a suitable location.

The end of the railroad line was a sparsely populated area of citrus and avocado groves, vineyards, and orchards known as Hollywood. De Mille rented half of Jacob Stein's barn on Selma Avenue to serve as his first studio. The other half of the barn was retained by the owner to lodge his horses and carriage. The ramshackle studio eventually became Paramount and, within a few years, Hollywood became the movie capital of the world.

The original version in 1913 was the first six-reel film. It was an enormous hit and, as a result, feature length films became the standard. Five years later De Mille remade *The Squaw Man*.

Cecil B. De Mille earned the title as "the greatest showman of them all." His speciality was the epic Biblical film which he populated with a cast of thousands. De Mille skillfully combined Biblical themes with lavish scenes of scantily clad women. He hoped to bring "sex to the masses" and succeeded. De Mille became one of the few directors to become as famous as the most popular movie stars.

Soft spoken, De Mille used a loudspeaker on the set to give instruction to the actors and the crew. He was a man of habit and for 30 years wore the same cashmere suits and old battered hat. Each day he drove to work in an old Locomobile which was once owned by General "Black Jack" Pershing, the commander of the American Expeditionary Force in World War I. Despite his frugality, De Mille liked to pass out gold-tipped cigarettes to reporters who visited the set. One of his most peculiar idiosyncrasies was his refusal to touched used currency. He constantly sent his assistant to the bank to get new bills.

De Mille's career had taken a downturn toward the end of the silent era, about the time he decided to make *The Squaw Man* once again — this time as a talkie. He began his third version in 1931. He had lost over a million dollars in the stock market crash of 1929 and was $150,000 in debt. His previous two films had been box-office failures in a city where you're only as good as your last film. In October, just prior to the beginning of shooting, he underwent an operation on his heel which had been splintered when he took a misstep off his yacht. Throughout the filming of *The Squaw Man*, he was in excruciating pain.

To make matters worse, Lupe Velez was on her worst behavior. Normally, Lupe was boisterous on the set but once the cameras started rolling she became totally professional. Perhaps, her unhappy love life was starting to take its toll. Whatever the reason, she was temperamental, foul-mouthed, and uncooperative. During her tirades she often threw props. De Mille, depressed and in constant pain, went through the motions while directing.

The film was shot on location in Hot Springs Junction, Arizona. The screenwriter was supposed to have been young John Huston, but he was replaced after making the then outrageous suggestion that the Indian roles be played by Native Americans. Lupe's costar was handsome Warner Baxter, at the time the highest paid actor in Hollywood. The dapper leading man had played Jay Gatsby in the original film version of *The Great Gatsby* and won an Oscar for best actor in 1929 for his portrayal of the Cisco Kid in *In Old Arizona*. He was cast in the role of the Mexican outlaw literally by accident. Raoul Walsh was scheduled to both direct and portray the Cisco Kid when a jack rabbit jumped through the windshield of his car, causing an accident which cost him an eye.

The Squaw Man opens in an English castle and ends in the Wild West. Baxter plays Jim Wynn, a British aristocrat who renounces his wife and travels to Arizona where he meets and falls in love with Naturich (Lupe Velez), the pig-tailed daughter of an Indian chief. After bearing his child, Naturich saves his life by killing evil cattle rustler Cash Hawkins (Charles Bickford). Wanted by the law, Naturich commits suicide and Baxter learns he has become an Earl. He returns to England with his half-breed child, Little Hal.

Lupe Velez earned favorable reviews for one of her most subdued performances. *Photoplay* noted: "With scarcely a dozen words of dialogue she holds our sympathy every second." Mordaunt Hall wrote in *The New York Times:* "Skillfully acted by a dozen good players, handsomely produced, and technically excellent, it makes an interesting entertainment. It is agreeable and expert melodrama."

The Squaw Man was a disappointment at the box office, losing $150,000 and De Mille was released from his contract at M-G-M. It appeared that his career as a major Hollywood director was over. De Mille was forced to accept a contract at his old studio, Paramount, for a fraction of his previous salary. He staged a miraculous comeback with his next film, *The Sign of the Cross*, and remained a top director until his death in 1959.

The Cuban Love Song (1931), was Lupe's next film, a

departure from her previous roles. Her last four films were remakes and Lupe felt she was being typecast. She later recalled: "Back about 1927 [sic], I did dramatic movies like *The Squaw Man* for Cecil B. De Mille and Tolstoy's *Resurrection*. That was the only sort of thing I did and I got so fed up that I said, 'If you give me one more dramatic thing—if I cry again in a picture, I quit!' I wanted to sing hot songs. I knew I was typed, but all the producers would say was, 'Lupe dear, you are not suited to comedy.'"

Ironically, after repeated successes in comedies, Lupe went to producers demanding a change. "Please, may I do drama. I think I am very good at crying. And they say, 'Lupe dear, you are not suited to drama!' This is typical of Hollywood."

The Cuban Love Song was a musical comedy with a story line lifted from *Madame Butterfly*. Lupe's leading man was Metropolitan Opera star Lawrence Tibbett, whose magnificent singing voice was perfect for his role although his wooden acting contrasted with Lupe's energetic performance. She deliberately up-staged Tibbett during the film but he accepted it with good humor and they became close friends.

The film marked Lupe's first teaming with Jimmy Durante. The combination proved so successful that they starred together three more times. She discovered quickly that no one could upstage Durante and she downplayed their scenes together. Durante, known as the Great Schnozzola, had his prominent proboscis insured by Lloyd's of London for a million dollars. His nose was so famous that he left its imprint in the cement in front of Grauman's Chinese Theater rather than the customary handprints.

Being teamed with Jimmy Durante could be hazardous to a star's career as Buster Keaton discovered. During the twenties Buster Keaton rivalled Chaplin as the cinema's greatest comedian. He directed and starred in some of the funniest films ever made including Sherlock Jr. and The General. Keaton was married to actress Norma Talmadge and lived in a huge mansion. His brother-in-law, producer Nicholas Schenck, convinced Keaton to give up his independent production company and join M-G-M. He lost his writers and crew, and his films at M-G-M were inferior to his previous work. Keaton began to drink heavily and his marriage collapsed.

Schenck, his ex brother-in-law, sabotaged Keaton's career by teaming him with Jimmy Durante in dismal films such as *The Passionate Plumber* and *What, No Beer?* The Great Stone Face proved no match for Durante in scene stealing. Keaton, now broke, was forced to live in a trailer on the M-G-M lot. The end came when studio head Louis B. Mayer asked Keaton to greet visitors. Keaton went to a baseball game instead and Mayer threw him off the lot, virtually ending his career in films. Keaton went on a drinking binge and was considered unhirable by the studios.

The Cuban Love Song has socialite Terry Burke (Lawrence Tibbett) and buddies O. O. Jones (Jimmy Durante) and Romance (Ernst Torrence) joining the Marines on a lark. They are stationed in Cuba where Burke crashes his car into the donkey cart of a peanut vendor, Nenita (Lupe Velez). They fight but soon fall in love and have an affair. When his tour of duty is over, Burke returns to California and marries his aristocratic sweetheart (Karen Morley). Ten years pass and Burke decides to return to Havana to see Nenita, only to learn she had died after bearing his son. Guilt-stricken, he returns to the United States with Nenita's child.

In *The New York Times*, critic Mordaunt Hall found: "The vivacious Lupe Velez . . . dances energetically; she also adds her voice to some of the interludes of melody and volleys away in Spanish."

At last Lupe had the opportunity to display her comic, singing, and dancing skills in a movie. One of the film's highlights was her lively rhumba number. Film historian Miles Krueger noted, "Velez has the chance to reveal her exquisite sensitivity as a serious actress in addition to her beauty and flair for fiery comedy."

Lupe followed *The Cuban Love Song* with *The Broken Wing* (1932), a return to drama, playing opposite debonair Melvyn Douglas (in only his fourth film) and good-natured Leo Carrillo. Based on Paul Dickey and Charles W. Goddard's 1920 Broadway play, it was previously filmed in 1923.

Carrillo plays Captain Innocencio, a Mexican bandit, who falls in love with the vivacious Lolita Farley (Lupe Velez) and tries to impress her with stolen presents. When an American aviator, Philip Marvin (Melvyn Douglas), crashes nearby she takes a hankering toward him, believing he is her long-awaited "King of Hearts." Jealous, the bandit, in his self-appointed roles of chief of police and judge, orders the flier's execution, but the gringo is saved at the last minute from the firing squad.

Lupe Velez's stormy personal life made her the subject of many magazine articles. The public couldn't seem to get enough of her. In January 1932, the *Satur-*

day Evening Post ran a feature entitled "A Redhead From Mexico." Interviewing Lupe was a difficult task because she couldn't sit still for more than a few seconds. She confessed that she was tired of Hollywood and might go to Europe. She also mentioned the possibility of going to New York to appear in *George White's Scandals* or the *Ziegfeld Follies*.

The *Post* interviewer, Frank Condon, called Lupe the linguistic marvel of the era. "Miss Velez now speaks perfect English, if you make certain natural allowances for her youth, inexperience, and the fact that she cannot speak English perfectly." Lupe claimed that the only curse word she ever used was "hell." "I am as dignified and dull as anyone," she said. No one believed her.

Lupe spoke of her various pets including two rare miniature Mexican dogs and a Great Dane, Eric the Great, which she nicknamed "Headache." The article noted that Lupe was probably the most versatile actress in films having played Chinese, Eskimos, Japanese, Indians, Hindus, Swedes, Malays, Mexicans, and French Canadians.

Condon learned that even conducting an interview with Lupe could erupt into violence. During their chat Lupe's comment that Greta Garbo was the most beautiful woman in the world put her at odds with a bystander and Lupe nearly came to blows with the man, who continued to contradict her opinions. Condon cut the interview short to avoid bloodshed.

Lupe's romances with Gary Cooper and John Gilbert had ended badly but she was never without male companionship for very long. She announced that she would reveal her new lover at the annual Mayfair Ball;

held each year on New Year's Eve at the Mayfair Club, it was the social event of the season—practically the only time all the major stars from the various studios were together under one roof.

The never-at-a-loss Lupe kept up the suspense by arriving at the ball alone. Then, at midnight, a tall, handsome, young actor named Randolph Scott appeared. *The Hollywood Reporter* wrote: "As though someone had suddenly flipped a switch, Lupe lit up like a proverbial Christmas tree. She melted into Randy's arms and, as far as the town knew, they were still arm-in-arm somewhere—all alone, together."

Scott had graduated from the University of North Carolina with a degree in engineering. He met Howard Hughes on a golf course and the maverick producer encouraged him to get into the movies. Louis B. Mayer saw his screen test and gasped, "He looks like an Adonis."

Lupe's happiness with Scott was short-lived as he moved in with Cary Grant. For the second time one of her beaus had left her for another man. The two actors lived together for nearly ten years in a Spanish style hacienda located high in the Hollywood Hills. So inseparable were Scott and Grant that they were nicknamed "Hollywood's Damon and Pythias," photographed as if they were a married couple. The fan magazines showed them in aprons washing dishes or making their side-by-side twin beds. Rumors circulated that Grant and Scott were lovers. The studio heads, nervous about how the gossip might affect the careers of two of their most promising leading men, discouraged the stories.

Although both men wed several times, each time their marriages broke up, they returned to live with one another. When Cary Grant was filming *Blonde Venus*, his costar Marlene Dietrich was asked what her feelings were about him. She replied, "I had no feelings. He was a homosexual." In fact, it was Cary Grant who was credited with coining the term "gay" in the classic 1938 screwball comedy, *Bringing Up Baby*, in a scene in which he wore a woman's dress. When asked what he was doing in a dress, he answered nonchalantly, "I've gone gay!"

11

Material Girl

For years Lupe, after becoming a big film star, had a yen to conquer Broadway. In the winter of 1932, she signed to star in Florenz Ziegfeld's latest extravaganza, *Hot-Cha!* Ziegfeld assembled an all star cast which included Bert Lahr, Buddy Rogers, and Eleanor Powell. The show opened on March 8, 1932, at the Ziegfeld Theater and ran for 119 performances.

Florenz Ziegfeld had been the toast of Broadway for over two decades. His *Follies* featured the most talented performers in American theater including W. C. Fields, Will Rogers, and Fanny Brice. Some of the most beautiful women in the world were Ziegfeld Girls including Lillian Lorraine, Anna Held, Olive Thomas, and Louise Brooks.

Well-known womanizer Florenz Ziegfeld had been wiped out in the stock market crash and was supported by his patient wife, actress Billie Burke. Whenever creditors came to his door, Ziegfeld fled down a fire escape to a waiting automobile.

Aging and in failing health, Ziegfeld wanted to produce one last great show. In order to finance *Hot-Cha!*,
Ziegfeld sought the backing of one of New York's most
notorious gangsters, "Dutch" Schultz. During the Depression it was common for underworld bigwigs to be
the "angels" backing Broadway shows because bootleg-
ging was one of the few profitable businesses.

By the time he was thirty-years old, Dutch Schultz
had amassed a fortune of over seven million dollars.
Born Arthur Flegenheimer in 1902, he changed his
name to Dutch Schultz after a member of the notorious nineteenth century Frog Hollow Gang. During
prohibition he prospered as a bootlegger despite selling
the worst needle beer in New York. After rival "Legs"
Diamond hijacked one of his beer trucks, Schultz ordered his gangland execution.

In the thirties, to improve his image, Schultz decided
to hire a public relations man after being indicted on
income tax evasion. He tried to pass himself off as a
family man and donated large amounts of money to
charity. Backing *Hot-Cha!* was one of the ways he
hoped to demonstrate that he was a legitimate
businessman.

Schultz career as a Broadway producer was short-
lived. In 1935, he planned to kill special prosecutor
Thomas Dewey because his crimebusting efforts
threatened Dutch's underworld empire. The mob realized that if Schultz carried out the hit, the heat put on
organized crime by the law enforcement agencies
would be unbearable. Murder Inc.'s new czar, Albert
Anastasia sent hitman Charles "The Bug" Workman to
pay Dutch a visit. On October 23, 1935, in the bath-

room of the Palace Chop House in Newark, New Jersey, Workman shot Dutch Schultz to death.

Mobsters were always hanging around the theater during the rehearsals of *Hot-Cha!* From the beginning, fiery Lupe kept the production in a constant state of upheaval. She hated being confined by her costumes and had the disconcerting habit of rehearsing in the nude. She made the trip from the hotel to the theater each night in a mink coat and slippers with nothing underneath.

Lupe developed a curious friendship with costar, Bert Lahr, who was intrigued by her unorthodox behavior. He recalled, "She couldn't laugh. She cackled like a duck. I'd say things under my breath to her on the stage and she'd start to cackle. Lupe never washed. When she'd go to the Mayfair or somewhere she'd just put on a dress. Nothing under it. Nothing. So when I'd be clowning with her on the stage and I'd notice her dirty hands I'd say, 'You've got your gloves on again.'"

Onstage Lupe would chew gum and let it hang out of the side of her mouth so Lahr could see it but the audience couldn't. It would break him up every time. He was amused by her eccentricities and attracted to her sensuality. Once, Lahr's girlfriend (and later wife) Mildred, who was insanely jealous of Lupe, fainted when he left her to rush through a revolving door to greet Velez. Lupe openly expressed her affection for Bert Lahr when she said, "I love him."

The show's minimal plot had Lahr masquerading as the world's most fearless matador. Lupe played his love interest, Conchita, a woman of questionable character. She sang three songs: "Conchita," "Say What I Wanna

Hear You Say," and the show-stopping "They All Need a Little Hot-Cha." Lupe was so identified with the role that she became known as the "Queen of the Hot-Cha." While the show received mixed reviews, most of Lupe's notices were positive. *The New York Times* described her gyrating dances as "fascinatingly disjointed."

Backstage, Lupe put on an even better show. Lupe watched the show through a crack and she laughed so loudly that she could be heard by the audience. Her makeup was caked so thick that someone observed, "[it] looks like a custard pie that has seen life."

Lupe justified her fun-loving ways: "These people who come to see me, they come for a good time. If I don't have a good time, they don't either. When I know they love me, I'm happy. Then they're happy, too. No, I never try to change myself. I couldn't be Garbo. But it would be so dull if we were all Garbos! People like her because she's quiet and so beautiful. They like me because I have pep. We must just be ourselves. Make the most of what you've got. But be sure to glorify the things you have. The quickest way to make other people tire of you is to get that slightly glazed expression that means you're looking at yourself."

Collier's magazine featured Lupe Velez in an article entitled "The Girl With One Talent." Because she was totally uninhibited, she was an interviewer's dream. Writer Elizabeth Dickson tried to define Lupe's unique appeal; "It isn't beauty. It isn't brains. It isn't ordinary charm. This thing called lure is a current that goes out from its possessor and brings back to her almost anything she wants. Take Lupe Velez for example. New York at this moment thinks this Mexican whirlwind tops the lure market by several miles. She never acted in her life and that's her secret. Fantastic? Yes, she's all of that and the despair of her press agent."

Dickson described Lupe's impact on the show: "The stage seems empty when she isn't on. . . . On she comes, and the topmost row in the balcony gets a shot in the arm. Talking, singing, dancing, imitating, this girl from over the border is having such a perfectly swell time herself that the gulf between the audience and performer closes up. This isn't technique. It's a gift."

There apparently was a childlike charm to Lupe which seemed to appeal to everyone. Men were attracted to her physically and women identified with her independence and spirit.

Lupe loved jewelry, saying, "I can't live without them. They make me feel alive." *The Hollywood Reporter* noted: "Everyone always said that the adorable, fiery Lupe looked like a Christmas tree when she dressed up. It was true. She loved real sparkling jewelry. In fact, over the years, she had bought herself drawersful of diamonds, sapphire, ruby, and emerald rings, necklaces, bracelets, earrings, and broaches. Frequently she was seen on-the-town all loaded down with gems."

In many ways, Lupe Velez was the original material girl. Her taste in jewelry was eclectic. On her left hand she wore a giant emerald cut diamond while on her right she had a plain horseshoe nail ring for good luck. She was constantly receiving jewels from her many male admirers. During *Hot-Cha!* a man came backstage and presented her with a gorgeous bracelet, two-and-a-half inches wide and encrusted with diamonds and twenty-one large rubies.

Lupe stared glassy-eyed at the bracelet. "I am mad about that bracelet, just mad. I have bracelets from here to here, but I never have enough." She looked at the beautiful bracelet she was already wearing. "I think I will give away that little one and get this," she said.

She was generous with her possessions, and during the run of the show she raffled off one of her fur coats to benefit members of the chorus.

James Cagney remembered arriving at a Beverly Hills party when Lupe drove up in a limousine. She wore an expensive full-length ermine coat but as soon as she saw the chinchilla coat on a socialite she quickly encountered, she knew she must have it. Lupe lifted up the sleeve of the coat to reveal several expensive bracelets on her arm. "You can have any of these you want but I want that coat," she told the woman. The socialite selected two of the most beautiful bracelets and the deal was done. Lupe casually put on the chinchilla and rolled up the ermine coat she had been wearing into a ball and threw it into the trunk of her car.

Hot-Cha! proved to be Florenz Ziegfeld's last show. Unhappy with the script and dismayed by Lupe's wild behavior, a weakened Ziegfeld contracted influenza. It developed into pneumonia and by the time *Hot-Cha!* opened, he was nearly comatose. Eventually, pleurisy set in and the great Ziegfeld died on July 22, 1932, not long after *Hot-Cha!* closed its run, after racking up a modest 119 performances, mainly, it turned out, on the shoulders of Lahr and Lupe.

Lupe collected men as easily as she collected gems and furs. Her latest catch was Winfield Sheehan, production chief and one of the founders of the Fox Studio. Sheehan was one of the most powerful and highly-paid executives in Hollywood, once earning twice as much in a year as M-G-M's more visible Louis B. Mayer.

A one-time crime reporter for a newspaper, Sheehan met William Fox while working as a secretary to the police commissioner. A powerfully built man, he physically protected Fox when he was threatened with bodily harm as a result of taking on the Motion Picture Patents Company. Fox rewarded him by making him an executive with his newly-formed, self-named studio.

An extravagant man who spared no expense in the pursuit of a woman he desired, Sheehan courted and married Maria Jeritza, the most beautiful and tempestuous grand opera star of the day. He built for her a miniature castle in Hidden Valley, furnished with art and antiques from all over the world.

Sheehan had an uncontrollable temper and refused to back down from even the biggest stars. After an argument with an inebriated Spencer Tracy, he locked the drunken star in a sound stage at the studio. In a fury, Tracy wrecked the entire set.

Winfield Sheehan hated criticism and each day rounded up all the copies of *The Hollywood Reporter* he could gather and started a bonfire. From his office he blissfully watched the smoke rise.

Lupe found the dynamic Sheehan very exciting. In his late forties, he maintained his firm physique with daily workouts at the Los Angeles Athletic Club. He had the reputation of throwing the best parties in Hollywood. Sheehan loved to gamble and played high-stakes faro regularly on the Rex, a twenty-four hour-a-day floating casino with a 250 foot glass enclosed gaming table. It was anchored out past the three mile limit off Santa Monica.

While she was in New York Lupe met the man who would make her forget about Winfield Sheehan. She was staying in a small hotel, just off Broadway, owned by Marion Davies and a favorite of M-G-M stars. Also a guest there was a young actor named Johnny Weissmuller. Lupe had always been attracted to physical men and Weissmuller was her ideal. He was twenty-five years old, six-foot-three, with a physique like a Greek god.

Before he became an actor, Johnny Weissmuller was, perhaps, the greatest swimmer in history. Born in what is now Romania, he was the son of a coal miner who died when Johnny was a child. In 1922, he became the first person to swim the hundred meter free-style in less than a minute. Over a period of eight years, from 1921 to 1929, Weissmuller never lost a race. He won three gold medals at the 1924 Olympics in Paris and added two more four years later in the summer games in Amsterdam. During his swimming career he set sixty-seven world records, some of which stand today.

Weissmuller was in training for the 1932 Summer Olympics in Los Angeles when he accepted $500 to pose for an underwear ad. At the time producers were conducting a nationwide search for a new face to play Tarzan in a M-G-M feature, *Tarzan, The Ape Man*. The producers spotted Weissmuller in the underwear advertisement and knew instantly that they had found their Tarzan.

Lupe first saw Johnny Weissmuller in the hotel lobby and promptly phoned his room. "This is Lupe Velez. I am on the floor below you. Will you come down and have a drink with me?"

Weissmuller readily accepted the invitation and spent the evening sipping pink champagne with Lupe. During their stay in New York, Lupe and Johnny were inseparable. "He is my type of man. I will love only this kind," Lupe gushed.

There was only one problem with the budding romance. Johnny Weissmuller was already married.

12

Tarzan

At first, Lupe and Johnny denied they were romantically involved. "It is not true," Lupe insisted. "If I am in love I will say it is true. Johnny and I are friends, that is all." When the newspaper reporters refused to believe their denials, the two took their case to the movie magazines. Lupe insisted she was not a homewrecker.

"I can't even look at a man without everybody saying I'm in love with him. One thing they can say is this, Lupe never broke up any home. I don't want anybody's husband. I didn't even know Johnny liked me. Then one day he said, 'Lupe, I love you. I just want to look at you.'

"I yell at Johnny. 'Go away and don't let me hear your voice. I never want to see you again.' Besides, Winnie Sheehan is my boyfriend.

"Let that Johnny Weissmuller go back to his wife. I don't want anything to do with him. Believe Lupe, she can't help it if handsome men say they love her, can she?"

Despite the denials, rumors of the romance persisted. Finally, Weissmuller's wife, socialite and dancer Bobbe Arnst, made the separation official in a *Screen Book* interview entitled "Tarzan Seeks a Divorce."

"Yes, Johnny and I are finished. He wants a Mexican divorce but I won't have it. We will get an honest-to-goodness California divorce, though, as soon as we can file the papers. Johnny is madly in love with Lupe Velez. I do not know whether or not she loves him or if they will get married but I've known about the affair for some time. I've tried to fight it out. It's no use, the gossips win. Marriage can't be victor in Hollywood.

"I've lost but I'll try to take it like a man, and if Lupe, or anyone else can make Johnny happier, I want him to have her. I loved him and did what I could but Hollywood was too much for us. It breaks my heart to lose my boy but I'll play the game, no matter what it costs me.

"It happened so suddenly that I was dumbfounded. While Johnny was in New York he wrote me long love letters almost every day and when he returned it was like another honeymoon. We had never been so happy with each other—not even when we were first married.

"One night after returning from a party he said without warning, 'I want a divorce.'

"'Why, Johnny. There must be a reason.'

"'No, only that I want to be free.'

"'He's such a big baby and so unbelievably naive.'"

Arnst claimed that Weissmuller didn't even know you had to hire a lawyer to get a divorce. He believed that you could obtain a divorce by just telling your spouse that you wanted one. When Arnst asked him to remove his personal possessions from her apartment, he asked, "What's the matter, haven't you got enough room for them?"

"When I saw a preview of *Tarzan* I knew Johnny would be besieged by millions of women, women who wanted him. I thought that the best way to hold him against them was to give him free rein. I wanted to go to New York with him but I knew I should not, so I stayed at home. I thought I could beat this game which Hollywood plays but now I admit I have lost.

"I have nothing against Lupe. She was very kind to me once, when I was ill in New York. I do not know if she even cares for Johnny in a big way but I am sure he is infatuated with her."

Johnny Weissmuller gave a different account of the reasons for the breakup of his marriage.

"I loved her [Arnst] at first but it began to fade when she always wanted to go everyplace I went. You see the trouble with Bobbe is that she always tells people I am a boy, that I don't know my own mind. She takes the credit for making up my mind for me. Well this time she can't do it. I'm finished.

"When I'm divorced from her I won't marry again. Gee, I'm scared of marriage. I'm scared of everything now."

Lupe threw a fit everytime she was depicted as a homebreaker. "It makes me sick when I hear the things she (Arnst) says about me." Lupe blamed Johnny for the situation and he was usually the victim of her tantrums.

"Poor Lupe is all burned up and sore at me," he admitted. When someone at poolside suggested that

Lupe had been responsible for the breakup, of Weissmuller's marriage, Lupe threw his clothes at Johnny and said, "I won't ever speak to you again."

She didn't keep her promise. In between pictures, she continued to see Weissmuller on a regular basis. Their studio, M-G-M, encouraged the romance because both stars were under contract and it was good publicity.

Lupe's next film was *Hombres en Mi Vida*, Columbia's Spanish language version of *Men in Her Life*.* Its director was William "One Shot" Beaudine, one of the most prolific in Hollywood history. He was "One Shot" because he rarely reshot a scene, even if it included an obvious mistake.

Lupe continued to make headlines with her off-screen antics. In 1932, she had a celebrated fight with actress Lilyan Tashman in the powder room of the Montmartre Cafe, a popular Hollywood lunch spot. Tashman was regarded as the personification of the sophisticated woman. Her father had been a clothing manufacturer and Tashman was universally recognized as the best dressed woman in Hollywood. She took pride in never wearing the same outfit twice and reportedly had more clothes than any other actress. She personally selected the wardrobe of her close friend, Greta Garbo, and was the first to accept the credit for making her "look as good as she could look."

Tashman, who was discovered by Florenz Ziegfeld, loved to be outrageous. Each afternoon she served her pet cat high tea. She bought the first white piano in

---

*Filmed in 1931 with Lois Moran, Charles Bickford, and Victor Varconi, and directed by William Beaudine.

Hollywood and made a fashion statement by tying a big blue satin ribbon around it. Tashman once greeted her guests at a tea dance while wearing sensuous red pajamas. She painted her dining room dark blue for one of her famous Easter Sunday brunches so the walls would contrast with her golden hair. Another time she required her guests to dress entirely in red and white. In honor of the occasion she painted everything in her Malibu home red and white. Even the toilet paper was color coordinated. Lilyan Tashman, with her throaty, insinuating voice and tongue-in-cheek humor, could be abrasive at times. She and Lupe were complete opposites and, in the case of the legendary Montmartre confrontation, they didn't attract. In spite of her sophisticated image, Tashman could hold her own in any cat fight. She was once charged with assault after beating up a woman she caught in husband Edmund Lowe's dressing room.

This time, however, Lilyan Tashman had met her match. Although she was much taller than Lupe, she had never encountered anyone like the Mexican wildcat. The women fought, clawed, and wrestled on the floor of the powder room. By the time they were separated, Lilyan Tashman no longer looked like the best dressed woman in Hollywood.

Tragically, Lilyan Tashman died two years later at thirty-four while being operated on for a brain tumor. At her funeral several people were hospitalized when a large tombstone was knocked over by the crush of people attempting to see the burial.

Lupe Velez had the reputation for throwing the wildest parties in Hollywood. One of her most memorable took place in August 1932. At the time Lupe was competing with her old rival, Clara Bow, to see who could throw the best soiree. Bow tried to woo guests with delicious fried chicken lunches, unlimited booze, and round-the-clock gambling, complete with a roulette wheel and poker tables. Lupe countered by hosting a nonstop two-day barbecue. Her favorite party trick was to spin around and pull her skirt over her head to reveal she didn't wear underwear. Reportedly, her seventy-five guests were treated to cockfights and stag movies.

Lupe's next feature was *Kongo,* (1932) a remake of Lon Chaney's *West of Zanzibar.* One of the best actors in Hollywood, Walter Huston, who had been in the stage version, starred opposite her, along with Conrad Nagel and Virginia Bruce, the new wife of John Gilbert. Blonde and shapely, Bruce had been discovered by director William Beaudine. He spotted her while she was taking a walking tour of the Fox Studio and signed the teenager to a $25 a week contract. Shortly after he broke up with Lupe Velez, John Gilbert met Virginia Bruce when they costarred in *Downstairs.* Bruce became one of the hottest actresses in Hollywood, once making fourteen films in a sixteen month period. It was Bruce who introduced Cole Porter's "I've Got You Under My Skin" in the film, *Born to Dance.*

The plot of *Kongo* was typical Hollywood melodrama. Lupe starred as Tula, the Portuguese mistress of Deadeye Flint (Walter Huston), a crippled madman ruler of an African colony. Embittered, he seeks revenge on the man responsible for crippling him. He is convinced that Ann (Virginia Bruce) is the daughter of his enemy and exacts his revenge by degrading and torturing her. Only after Ann becomes a prostitute does he learn that she is really his own daughter.

Huston's scenes with Lupe Velez were noteworthy for their sadistic violence. In one scene he punishes Lupe for her infidelity by twisting her tongue with a wire while her lover is thrown to the crocodiles in a swamp.

"Lupe Velez appears as a Portuguese wench" was the extent of her mention in Mordaunt Hall's review of this "audible scene shocker" in *The New York Times.*

Returning to comedy, Lupe next starred in *The Half-Naked Truth*, directed by Gregory La Cava in 1932. W. C. Fields said that La Cava had the best comedy mind in Hollywood—excluding himself. Her costars were Lee Tracy, best remembered for his fast-talking nasal delivery, and Frank Morgan, long before becoming The Wizard of Oz.

Lupe plays Teresita, a performer in a sideshow which is so unsuccessful that the fat woman weighs only 112 pounds and the strong man is too weak to eat. After loquacious publicity agent Jimmy Bates (Lee Tracy) two-times her for a blonde, the hot-tempered Teresita goes after him with a gun. When the carnival is raided by the police, the two go to New York where he hopes to make her an overnight celebrity. Bates cooks up a scheme to pass Teresita off as Princess Exotica, an escaped harem beauty, and tricks Ziegfeld-like Broadway producer Farrell (Frank Morgan) into casting her in his new revue. Teresita becomes a sensation but Bates, no longer needed, is fired. Eventually she is replaced and ends up with Bates back at the carnival where they started.

The Half-Naked Truth was one of Lupe's most successful comedies. Film historian Roger Niven called her performance "one of the lewdest on film."

Hot Pepper, (1933) Lupe's next film, costarred her with Victor McLaglen and Edmund Lowe, recreating their roles as bickering Marine sergeants Flagg and Quirt made famous in the 1926 silent classic, *What Price Glory?* and later *The Cock-Eyed World.*

Big, rugged Victor McLaglen was a star for four decades. The son of an Anglican bishop, McLaglen ran away from home at an early age. He took various jobs including carnival barker, professional wrestler, and gold prospector. His most unusual job was as physical culture advisor to the Rajah of Akolkot in India. Because of his magnificent body, he modeled for statues of Hercules and Adonis. McLaglen was a skilled boxer and a contender for the heavyweight championship. In 1909, he fought champion Jack Johnson for the title, the bout went the distance and ended in a no decision. Following his boxing career, he turned to acting and in 1935, won an Oscar for his portrayal of Gypo Nolan in The Informer. Notorious for his extreme right-wing political views, he was Commandant of the Hollywood Czars, a pro-Nazi organization.

A rowdy comedy, *Hot Pepper* tells the story of a Latin entertainer named Pepper (Lupe Velez, who received third billing) who is discovered as a stowaway. The owner of the ship, Flagg (Victor McLaglen) is a bootlegger who owns a nightclub. He signs Pepper to perform at his club and she is a big success. His old rival from the Marine Corps, Harry Quirt (Edmund Lowe), opens his own nightspot and uses his wits to steal Lupe away from the slow-thinking Flagg. In the end the two men decide to rejoin the Marines.

"The principal charmer in this case is impersonated by Lupe Velez, who displays a good measure of audacity, recklessness and extraordinary vitality," *The New York Times* found. "The role is that of Pepper, who, one might hazard, is well named. It looks as though Miss Velez wanted to outdo Lili Damita's performance in the enormously successful production, *The Cock-Eyed World*."

Lupe's final film of 1933 was an oddity titled *Mr. Broadway*. The idea of then New York *Daily News* columnist Ed Sullivan, it was filmed in various Manhattan nightclubs and featured numerous celebrities including Jack Benny, Jack Dempsey, Bert Lahr, and Jack Haley, as well as Lupe, who is seen hobnobbing at the Central Park Casino.

Ed Sullivan began his career as a sportswriter. In 1931, he began writing a Broadway column for *The Graphic*, a tabloid which Sullivan called, "a step removed from pornography." The next year Sullivan was given his own radio show and asked Jack Benny, who was performing at a local nightclub, to be his first guest. Benny introduced him to other entertainers and Sullivan got the idea for *Mr. Broadway*.

In March 1933, Lupe returned to Broadway to star with Jimmy Durante and Hope Williams in the revue, *Strike Me Pink*, which opened at the Majestic Theater and ran for 122 performances. *Strike Me Pink*, like *Hot-Cha!*, was financially backed by an underworld figure. "Waxey" Gordon was a bootleg syndicate head in New York who put up $150,000 to back the show. At the time Gordon was considered public enemy number two (behind "Legs" Diamond). During the gang wars Gordon ingeniously lowered a bomb down the chimney of rival gangster (and Broadway producer) Dutch

Schultz's headquarters, nearly killing a young hoodlum named "Bugsy" Siegel.

According to Robert Baral, in his book *Revue*, Lupe "imitated Gloria Swanson and Marlene Dietrich, among others, and teamed with Durante for some funny skits."

In *Strike Me Pink*, Lupe had the irritating habit of bumping hips with Durante. One night Durante put a monkey wrench in his pocket and when Lupe bumped him she almost broke her hip. Enraged, she reached into his pocket and grabbed the wrench. With murderous intent, she chased Durante off the stage, down the steps, and through the audience, which believed it was part of the show and roared as Lupe tried to brain him with the wrench. The chase ended when Durante, in self defense, threw Lupe into the orchestra pit.

Two highlights of the revue were Lupe's song "Love and Rhythm" and the skit, Ultra Modern. *The New York Times* wrote of the incendiary Lupe: "She dances wantonly and some of her seductive gestures might be, if made by a less skillful artiste, a little abashing."

13

A Rocky Marriage

Lupe Velez and Johnny Weissmuller were secretly married on October 8, 1933, in Las Vegas. The wedding, which occurred at four o'clock in the morning, was performed without fanfare by a local justice of the peace. Returning to Hollywood, the two denied they were married, and three weeks passed before Lupe confirmed they were newlyweds. "It was my own business. I felt like saying I wasn't married, and now I feel like saying I am married."

Johnny Weissmuller moved into Lupe's Spanish style mansion on North Rodeo Drive in Beverly Hills. As a wedding present, Weissmuller gave Lupe a thirty-four-foot schooner which he christened the Santa Guadalupe. For Christmas, he bought her two hairless Mexican puppies and a diamond and ruby wristwatch. Lupe was more practical and gave her husband a pair of boxing gloves which were inscribed: "Darling, so you can punch me if I leave you." Weissmuller would need the boxing gloves to defend himself during the marriage.

The fan magazines carried numerous stories on how Tarzan would finally tame the wild Lupe. On January 24, 1934, less than four months after their wedding, the couple announced the first of their many separations. They had a serious fight over their different lifestyles. He was a day person while Lupe was a night owl. Months later, Lupe and Johnny patched up their differences and reconciled.

Lupe downplayed their fighting. "Fight? We all do. Johnny and I may fight, but no more than the rest of Hollywood. They call each other and darling in public, and then go home and smack each other in private. When Johnny and I get sore, we get sore no matter where we are! The way to be happy through marriage is to fight once a week, maybe more."

Lupe didn't need any particular provocation to fight as she explained, "Then for no reason I punch him right on the nose. He jumps up and says, 'Mama, you hit me.' and I say, 'Darling, I am so sorry. Hit me back.' and he says, 'Never mind, honey, you couldn't help yourself.' "

When Lupe made her public appearance tours around the country, Johnny Weissmuller sometimes joined her. In the spring of 1934, she was touring on the Loew's vaudeville circuit when Weissmuller met her in Cleveland. That night there was a melee in their hotel room. The police were called by guests who feared that Tarzan was beating the life out of the tiny Lupe. Lupe emerged from the room unscathed. "Take a look. See if you can find a black and blue one. He did not punch me. Let the world get used to my Johnny and me." Apparently, Weissmuller didn't fare so well in the fracas.

Their battling got to be so commonplace that it was news when they didn't fight. One publication ran a photo showing Lupe and Johnny smiling across the table at one another at the Hawaiian Paradise Club, a popular nightspot. The caption read: "What's wrong with this picture? Usually blows and angry words were flying between the movies' handsome Tarzan Johnny Weissmuller and his off-and-on-again wife Lupe Velez."

Weissmuller fared little better during their lovemaking. Lupe's was so ferocious that Johnny looked like a wildcat had attacked him. He arrived on the Tarzan set, his magnificent body covered with strawberry-size hickeys, scratches, and annular bites on his pecs. The studio had to use extensive body makeup before he was ready to shoot.

Although Lupe thought nothing of beating Johnny to a pulp, she was protective of him being abused by others. One night a customer at Ciro's tried to pick a fight with Weissmuller. Johnny shrugged off the incident but Lupe began punching the man, yelling, "You big ape! You leave my man alone!"

Both Lupe and Johnny made light of his role as Tarzan. Weissmuller remarked, "It was like stealing. There was swimming and I didn't have much to say. How can a guy climb trees, say, 'Me Tarzan, you Jane," and make a million?"

Lupe defended her broken English. "Everybody says, 'Why don't you learn better English, Lupe dear?' So I answer, 'I was married to a guy who can only say, 'Me

Tarzan, you Jane!' How can I learn English from him?"

In 1934 Lupe faced a crisis from an unexpected source. Sacramento district attorney Neil McAllister was conducting an investigation of the Communist influence in Hollywood, foreshadowing the Hollywood witchhunts of the forties and fifties which led to the blacklisting of dozens of actors, writers, and directors.

For some reason McAllister named nearly every Mexican star in Hollywood in the probe including Lupe Velez, Ramon Novarro, and Dolores Del Rio. Johnny Weissmuller immediately came to his wife's defense. "Why Lupe doesn't even know what Communism means," he said. The public believed him and the investigation was dropped.

Even after she married Johnny Weissmuller, Lupe's thoughts were never far from Gary Cooper. Privately she admitted, "Gary's the only man I really love. There will not be him again." When Cooper starred in a film version of Ernest Hemingway's *A Farewell to Arms*, Lupe and Johnny attended the premiere. Lupe sat right behind Cooper, who was with the Countess di Frasso, and loudly praised his performance throughout the film.

With Lupe Velez out of the picture, the Countess di Frasso was determined to snare Cooper, the most eligible bachelor in town. Unfortunately, it seemed every other woman in Hollywood had the same idea. Tallulah Bankhead returned to Hollywood after years on the London stage for the sole purpose to, in her own words, "Fuck that divine Gary Cooper."

Bankhead had come from one of Alabama's most distinguished families. Her grandfather was a senator, her uncle was a congressman, and her father, William

Bankhead, became Speaker of the House. A city in Alabama was named Tallulah in honor of his daughter.

Unlike most stars, Tallulah Bankhead welcomed scandals. She relished stealing rivals' lovers, both male and female. With no warning she would strip in public. She openly admitted using cocaine. She said, "Cocaine isn't habit forming, darling. I ought to know. I've been taking it all my life."

Not everyone appreciated Bankhead's wicked wit. Actor Walter Slezak said, "Listening to her constant talk was like Chinese water torture." Composer Howard Dietz remarked, "A day away from Tallulah was like a month in the country." Even the formidable Joan Crawford was intimidated by Bankhead. "We were fascinated by her, but we were scared to death of her, too," she said.

Bankhead had her own way of dealing with rivals. When she learned that Marlene Dietrich sprinkled her hair with gold dust to make it lighter, she responded, "I'm going to do her one better. I'm going to sprinkle gold dust in my pubic hair."

She called the Countess di Frasso, "nothing but an old whore," the Countess retaliated by throwing wine in her face. The Countess was unable to keep Tallulah Bankhead away from Gary Cooper. Bankhead finally got her opportunity to seduce Cooper when they co-starred in *Devil and the Deep*. Bankhead was seen chasing Cooper into his dressing room and the next day she bragged about her one night stand. Mission accomplished, she was no longer interested in Gary Cooper.

One person still very much interested in Cooper was the Countess di Frasso. For a time she was the house guest of Mary Pickford at Pickfair. The Countess told

Pickford she was only going to stay for a day or two but, like the man who came to dinner, it appeared she would never leave. Pickford's husband, Buddy Rogers, learned that life with the Countess was never dull. "It was champagne and caviar. She lived it up good," he recalled. Pickford was less patient. She asked the Countess, "What about you and that outsized cowboy of yours?"

Pickford concocted a plan to reclaim her house. In September 1932, Pickford suggested that she, the Countess, and Gary Cooper sail for Italy. At the last minute Pickford received a telegram that she would have to remain in Hollywood to begin work on a new movie. Of course, the telegram was spurious, Pickford's way of ridding herself of the unwanted house guest. The Countess di Frasso and Gary Cooper went ahead with the trip.

When she returned, the Countess moved into her own mansion on North Bedford Drive. For her house warming party she had a boxing ring constructed in her garden. Among the guests were Clark Gable, Marlene Dietrich, Fred Astaire, Loretta Young, and Fredric March. The boxing matches were extremely bloody which seemed to please the Countess. Ironically, the Countess di Frasso replaced Mary Pickford as Holly-wood's leading hostess.

The Countess became a media celebrity. She pre-ferred to be interviewed in bed. At the right moment she sprang from under the covers, wearing a transpar-ent nightgown which revealed her voluptuous figure.

She secretly installed a dictaphone under the sofa in the front hall. After the guests were gone she replayed the record and was able to learn details about various stars' sex lives. No secret was safe with her and she loved to stir up feuds. The secret recording device backfired when she overhead John Barrymore making derogatory comments about herself. The Countess was so angry that she smashed the record into a thousand pieces.

In July 1933, the Countess di Frasso announced that she was divorcing the Count. Everyone realized that the reason for the divorce was so she would be free to marry Gary Cooper. Lupe howled when she heard the news, "Gary got himself into a big fix this time."

All this was not lost on Gary Cooper. While the Countess was less dangerous than Lupe, Cooper found it even harder to free himself from her clutches. The Countess' announcement did not have the effect she desired. In fact, it drove Gary Cooper right into the arms of a beautiful, young starlet named Veronica Balfe.

Like the Countess, Veronica Balfe came from a privileged background. She attended exclusive eastern finishing schools and was poised, elegant, and aloof. David O. Selznick spotted her at a party and signed her to a contract. She landed a small part in *King Kong*. In the movie the lovesick Kong mistook her for Fay Wray. When he realized his mistake he unceremoniously threw her off the top of a building. Preview audiences found the scene so disturbing that it was cut from the film.

Veronica Balfe was only twenty when she met Gary Cooper. Despite her aristocratic bearing, she was called Rocky by her friends. Thanks to his involvement with the Countess di Frasso, Cooper had acquired a taste for expensive things and he fell deeply in love with Rocky.

Cooper told reporters, "She is a wonderful girl, a beautiful girl any man would be proud to win as a wife. Rocky is the ideal girl for me. She can ride, shoot, and do all the things I like to do."

Cooper's studio disapproved of his relationship with the Countess di Frasso and encouraged his romance with Rocky. In desperation, the Countess invited Cooper on a safari to India but he declined the invitation. On November 6, 1933, Gary Cooper and Veronica Balfe announced their engagement. Rocky proudly displayed the beautiful fifteen-carat engagement ring Gary had given her.

Seven weeks later, on December 15, they quietly married. Rocky couldn't explain how she had succeeded where so many other women had failed. "I don't know how I snared him. He was ready, I guess. I didn't use a lariat."

Although she was already married to Johnny Weissmuller, Lupe Velez did not take the news of Gary Cooper's wedding well. From the first time they were introduced, Lupe Velez and Rocky Cooper detested one another. Lupe bitterly recalled their first meeting, "He introduced us in a nightclub. Sandra Shaw [Rocky's stage name] was who he said she was, an inspiring actress. Ha! I didn't swallow that one for I could see the way she looked at him and how she turned her back on me."

It seemed that everytime the two women met they nearly came to blows. One memorable confrontation occurred at Newark Airport. The Coopers were return-

ing from a vacation at Southampton when they ran
into Lupe Velez and Johnny Weissmuller at the airport. Lupe, angered at the sight of Cooper with another woman, made a scene. A photographer spotted
them and asked the newlywed couples to pose together
for a photo. Lupe refused, saying, "I'm happily married
and so is he. I wouldn't pose with him. Besides, he's no
oil painting himself, that one."

The next time they met the result was even more
volatile. Shortly after the wedding, Lupe Velez ran into
the Coopers at the Trocadero nightclub. Rocky refused
to acknowledge Lupe's presence and Velez responded
by throwing a drink into her face. Cooper grabbed
Lupe and held her tightly until her anger subsided.
There was Gary Cooper holding back Lupe Velez who
was kicking and screaming.

It was just like old times.

14

Hollywood Party

In August 1934, Lupe Velez and Johnny Weissmuller attended a formal dinner dance at the Little Club. Also attending were Gary and Rocky Cooper and the Countess di Frasso. For the first time Lupe Velez, Rocky Cooper and Dorothy di Frasso were under the same roof and anything could happen. Lupe remembered what occurred next:

"I was married then and the socialite [Rocky Cooper] needed someone in her corner. Gary's grandmother [the Countess] was the threat. She was available and very rich. She had the nerve to come into a restaurant and embarrass Rocky Cooper. So suddenly she [Rocky] was nice to Lupe."

Once again a photographer asked to take a shot of the Coopers and Weissmullers together. Lupe resisted but he persisted, and she grudgingly agreed to pose with the Coopers. The photo was widely published. Lupe, Johnny, and Rocky were all smiles but Gary looked uneasy.

Lupe soon discovered why Rocky Cooper was suddenly nice to her. Rocky invited Lupe and the Countess for lunch at the Mocambo and brought with her a pair of emerald cufflinks which the Countess had given Gary as a present. Rocky threw them at the Countess and said, "Gary wanted you to have these back. He has no use for them now." As hoped, Lupe sided with Rocky in the matter.

It was Lupe Velez who took the brunt of the Countess' wrath. "That Velez woman has no place in society," she fumed. "I was so sure Veronica Balfe would be more receptive. Instead she sides with that Mexican woman."

The Countess di Frasso was not easily put off. She encountered the Coopers at a fashionable restaurant, the Vendome. The Countess was holding a puppy that had been a gift from Gary Cooper. Gary spoke politely to the Countess but Rocky refused to look at her. The situation became awkward as the Countess wouldn't leave and the Coopers didn't ask her to sit down at their table. The Countess stood there for forty-five minutes before finally departing.

In retaliation for the snub, the Countess tried to socially ostracize Rocky Cooper. When that didn't work she decided to take more drastic measures. She hired a voodoo priest to stick pins in a waxed likeness of Rocky Cooper. Ultimately, the Countess admitted defeat. "I loved Gary and will always be his friend," she lamented.

The Countess di Frasso turned her attention to another handsome young actor, Cary Grant. She hoped to transform him into a sophisticated gentleman as she had previously with Gary Cooper. When he arrived in

Hollywood, Cary Grant was not the debonair character he portrayed in the movies. Born Archie Leach, he was the son of a Cockney clothes presser. His mother was committed to a mental institution when he was ten years old. Before he came to Hollywood he worked various odd jobs including being an acrobat, tumbler, clown, eccentric dancer, and mind reader. Perhaps his oddest job was as a stilt-walking advertisement at Coney Island. His film debut was playing a cuckolded javelin thrower in This Is The Night.

His frugality was legendary. Each night he would count the eggs in his refrigerator and draw a red ring around the milk bottle to make sure none of the servants ate any of the food. The Countess helped refine Cary Grant just as she had Gary Cooper. She assisted him in selecting his wardrobe and soon he was regarded as the best dressed man in Hollywood.

Still, it was difficult for the Countess to be in Hollywood with a married Gary Cooper. She announced that she was returning to Italy to introduce greyhound racing to the country, after throwing a memorable costume party at her Beverly Hills mansion. The Countess then sailed for Italy amid much fanfare. She would return.

In 1934, Lupe Velez signed a new contract with M-G-M and was hopeful she would be given choicer roles. Her first under the contract, *Laughing Boy*, seemed promising on the surface. It was adapted from a Pulitzer Prize-winning novel by Oliver La Farge. The film was shot on location on a Navajo reservation in Arizona.

The director of *Laughing Boy* was Hollywood veteran W. S. Van Dyke. Woodbridge Strong Van Dyke II was the son of a superior court judge in San Diego. Van Dyke worked as a lumberjack, prospector, and mercenary before he came to Hollywood. He served his apprenticeship under D. W. Griffith and played several roles in *Intolerance*. His career was going nowhere and was down to his last thirty-five cents when he sold a script to Fox. His luck changed and he became a prolific director at M-G-M with such films as *Trader Horn* and Lupe's *The Cuban Love Song*. He also directed Johnny Weissmuller in his first film, *Tarzan, The Ape Man*.

Playing opposite Lupe was fellow Mexican Ramon Novarro. One of thirteen children, Novarro was a second cousin to actress Dolores Del Rio. He fled in 1914 during the Mexican Revolution and worked as a singing waiter until he broke into the movies, starring in numerous silent epics including *The Four Horsemen of the Apocalypse, Scaramouche*, and *The Prisoner of Zenda*. His most famous role was as the title character in the original *Ben-Hur*. Known as "Ravishing" Ramon, he was Rudolph Valentino's greatest rival. Women fainted at the sight of his bare chest. What the public didn't know at the time was that Ramon Novarro, the heartthrob of millions of women, was a homosexual.

When talkies replaced silent pictures, Novarro's Mexican accent and high-pitched singing voice were considered liabilities. *Laughing Boy* would be one of Novarro's last starring roles. Wealthy from shrewd real estate investments, Novarro lived alone in semi-retirement on a fifty-acre ranch near San Diego. For a time he owned a house designed by Frank Lloyd Wright. Novarro had the interior decorated entirely in black fur and silver and whenever he had a dinner party, he instructed guests to dress only in black, white, and silver.

In 1966, he made headlines by suing the United States government for 57 million dollars for back rent on a piece of property which had been deeded to his grandfather by the Mexican President Juarez. Due to the change in course of the Rio Grande River, the land was now in American territory.

Novarro made an occasional film over the years and was back in the headlines for the last time in 1968, the victim of one of the most bizarre and brutal murders in Hollywood history. On Halloween, his nude, blood-spattered body was found in his Hollywood Hills home. Novarro's arms and legs were bound with an electrical cord and the letter "N" was carved into his neck. A broken silver-headed and ivory cane which had been used in the beating was placed across his legs and a condom was put in his hand. Reportedly, a black art deco dildo, which had been given to him by Rudolph Valentino, was rammed down his throat. Scrawled on the mirror was a message: "Us girls are better than fagots." The police apprehended two male hustlers who were convicted of the murder. Robbery was the apparent motive for the brutal slaying. It was rumored that Novarro kept large amounts of cash hidden in his house. The killers had escaped with only $45 in cash.

In *Laughing Boy*, as in *The Squaw Man*, Lupe was cast to play an Indian maiden, Slim Girl. Ramon Novarro portrayed her lover, a Navajo brave named Laughing Boy. The minimal plot has Lupe leaving the reservation to attend the white man's school. Returning to her native home, she is accidentally killed by an errant arrow meant for a white man whom childhood sweetheart Novarro believes has wronged her. Incredibly, this tearjearker was mutilated by the censors to appease the newly constituted Legion of Decency. The film never had a Manhattan opening, premiering in Brooklyn and went unreviewed in *The New York Times*.

In *The M-G-M Story*, author John Douglas Eames described it this way: "Every prolific director has made at least one he'd like to forget. *Laughing Boy* was W. S. Van Dyke's. . . . Mexican stars Ramon Novarro in the mis-title role, and Lupe Velez as his wigwam warmer, tried in vain to act like Indians. Audiences had plenty of seats to put their coats on."

For her next project, Lupe was loaned out to her old studio, United Artists, for *Palooka* (1934), a boxing movie based on the popular Ham Fisher comic strip. Once again, she was teamed with Jimmy Durante, in the role of Knobby Walsh, Joe Palooka's fight manager. Joe Palooka was played by Stu Erwin who specialized in portraying slow-thinking yokels. Others in the cast included Robert Armstrong, best remembered as the foolhardy film producer in *King Kong*, and William Cagney (Jimmy's lookalike younger brother). Also in the cast was sultry Thelma Todd, the famed "Hot Toddy" who a year later died under mysterious and still unsolved circumstances (although it was speculated that the mob was involved since Lucky Luciano was one of her lovers and had an eye on the popular restaurant she owned).

In *Palooka*, Lupe plays femme fatale Nina Madero, the self-proclaimed "wrecker of champions." This siren has already ruined the career of ex-champion Al McSwatt (Cagney) and then sets her sights on young

With Edmund Lowe and Victor McLaglen in *Hot Pepper* (1933).

Lupe Velez and Ramon Novarro as star-crossed lovers in *Laughing Boy* (1934).

Johnny Weissmuller, Olympic swimming champion and the movies' most famous Tarzan, had a stormy five-year marriage to Lupe Velez.

The hilarious egg-breaking scene with Laurel and Hardy was the highlight of *Hollywood Party* (1934). Tom Herbert is the bartender.

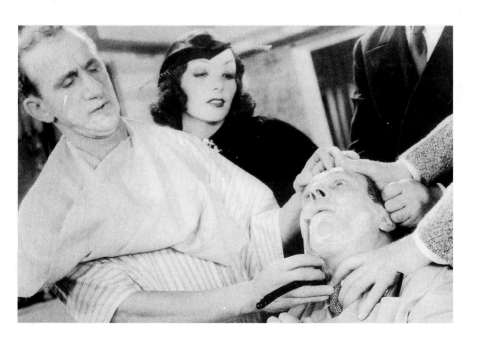

Watching Jimmy Durante giving a close shave in *Strictly Dynamite* (1934).

Lupe's love of jewelry is evident in this photo with Donald Woods.

With Leon Errol in *The Girl From Mexico* (1939), the first of eight "Mexican Spitfire" movies.

Lupe Velez as Carmelita and Leon Errol as Uncle Matt in *Mexican Spitfire* (1939).

In a vibrant dance number from *Six Lessons From Madame La Zonga* (1941).

With Forrest Tucker, Lloyd Bridges and Bruce Bennett in *Honolulu Lu* (1942).

The "Great Profile," John Barrymore, costarred with Lupe in his last film, *Playmates* (1942).

With Walter Reed and Lyle Talbot in *Mexican Spitfire's Elephant* (1942).

With Leon Errol and Zasu Pitts in *Mexican Spitfire at Sea*
(1942).

With Eddie Albert in the baseball comedy, *Ladies' Day*
(1943).

With Leon Errol in *Mexican Spitfire's Blessed Event* (1943).

contender Joe Palooka. She lures Palooka away from his sweetheart (Mary Carlisle) and nearly destroys his boxing career before he comes to his senses. The movie provided Jimmy Durante with what would become his signature song, "Inka-Dinka-Doo."

In 1934, Lupe Velez and Jimmy Durante were both in the stellar *Hollywood Party*. Originally, *Hollywood Party* was conceived by Buster Keaton as an all-star parody of *Grand Hotel*. Eventually, Keaton was dropped from the project by M-G-M, and the studio decided to use the film as a showcase for its major stars. The cast was to include Clark Gable, Joan Crawford, Jean Harlow, and Johnny Weissmuller, but none of these stars appeared in the film. The joke in the movie industry was that M-G-M gave a party and no one showed up.

From the beginning, *Hollywood Party* was star-crossed. Three directors were fired before the film even got underway. Actor Eddie Quillan remembered, "I think we had every director on the lot. And when it was finished, nobody wanted the credit." In fact, when the film was released, the directors went uncredited.

Hollywood Party, with a surprisingly forgettable score by the estimable team of Richard Rodgers and Larry Hart, most of which was cut from the released version, took so long to complete that it was said that it was made under three Presidents.

The cast of *Hollywood Party*, while not all-star, was still pretty respectable: Laurel and Hardy, the Three Stooges, Polly Moran, Charles Butterworth, Jack "Baron Munchausen" Pearl, Eddie Quillan, even Mickey Mouse. An incident occurred during shooting which was pivotal in the career of Arthur Treacher.

The English actor, at the time a minor player, was cast as a butler in the picture. Between takes, Lupe Velez tried to make small talk and commented that her husband was as tall as the six-foot-three Treacher. Unimpressed, Treacher said, "Really," in a disdainful manner. The director overheard the conversation and suggested that Treacher use the crusty butler character in the film. As a result, Treacher became Hollywood's quintessential gentleman's gentleman.

Hollywood Party satirizes the Tarzan films which Lupe's husband, Johnny Weissmuller, had made famous. Jimmy Durante dreams he is Schnarzan, the king of the Hollywood jungle films. In the opening scene Lupe, as the Jaguar Girl, burlesques her real-life relationship with Weissmuller. Schnarzan's popularity is waning because the lions he fights in his films are old and toothless. Explorer Baron Munchausen (Jack Pearl) is bringing a shipment of ferocious lions from Africa and Schnarzan hopes to buy them. Standing in his way is rival jungle star, Liondora.

Schnarzan decides to throw a party in honor of the Baron, but has a fight with Lupe and refuses to invite her, fearing that she'll make a scene. "You get too rough for a party," he tells her. Outraged, Lupe does a delicious imitation of Durante and calls him a "dirty snake in the bush."

Lupe crashes the party by climbing over the wall. Liondora, who wants the lions for his movies, comes disguised as a duke. The Baron Munchausen makes a spectacular entrance, carried in by a gorilla named Ping Pong, which he claims is the son of King Kong. Lupe meets a millionaire and demonstrates what she's going to do to Schnarzan by choking him. When the mil-

lionaire tries to get fresh with her, she flips him over
her shoulder. Outside Schnarzan's mansion, the Three
Stooges have a brief bit as autograph hounds. In a
funny scene, a group of scientists attending the party
compare the Stooges' heads to prehistoric man. They
declare that Curly's noggin is a particularly fine example of primitive man.

Women at the party scream when they see a mouse
which turns out to be Mickey Mouse. Mickey is
featured in an animated sequence entitled "Red Hot
Chocolate Soldiers" which is regarded as one of the
finest examples of an early Disney Technicolor
cartoon.

Laurel and Hardy arrive, claiming that the Baron
had bought the lions from them. They were paid with a
worthless check made out for fifty-thousand tiddly-
winks. The lions break loose and Schnarzan wrestles
with one on the stairs. At this point, Durante wakes up
and realizes he had fallen asleep while reading *Tarzan
the Untamed* and the party had all been a dream. At the
end of the movie, Durante gets ready to attend a real
party thrown by Lupe Velez which, all things considered, would no doubt have been more interesting than
the one we've seen in the film.

The highlight of *Hollywood Party* was a hilarious egg-
breaking between Lupe Velez and Laurel and Hardy.
The *New York Herald Tribune* review describes the
action: "Miss Velez kicks off her dainty golden slipper.
After a spirited debate, Mr. Laurel wins the right from
Mr. Hardy to return the lady's footwear, whereupon
she throws it at him. Mr. Hardy then impulsively takes
off his own slipper and is about to crack it over her
head when his companion interferes. At which Miss

Velez, seated at a bar, upon which a bowl of eggs is handy, deftly breaks an egg in two, and pours the contents in the shoe held by the amazed Mr. Hardy. This naturally leads to the breaking of more eggs . . . in a fierce battle for supremacy."

The Hollywood Reporter called it: "One of the funniest sequences seen in many a day. It had last night's preview audience rolling in the aisles and actually sobbing with laughter. The sequence is worth the price of admission . . . the greatest and longest bellylaugh scene for a long time."

There was some tension on the set between the Three Stooges and comedian Ted Healy. At the time the act was billed as Ted Healy and his Three Stooges, and Moe and Curly Howard and cousin Larry Fine were merely foils for headliner Healy, a popular vaudevillian whose confident style influenced Bob Hope and Milton Berle.

Originally, there had been four stooges. The fourth, Pansy Sanborn, played the xylophone. When Pansy left, three stooges remained: Moe, Larry, and Shemp. Moe Howard had toured the country as a Shakespearean actor and Larry Fine was a violinist before they became stooges. Moe's brother, Shemp, quit the act after a disagreement with Healy, who insisted on a separate dressing room from the stooges. Shemp's younger brother, Jerry, was auditioned to replace him. Jerry, who had curly blonde hair and a moustache, was a ballroom dancer with little experience in comedy. Healy initially rejected him, saying that he was too handsome and not funny enough to be a stooge. Healy remarked that Jerry was too normal for the act. Shemp suggested that his brother shave off his beautiful golden locks. Jerry Howard became Curly, who quickly became the most popular stooge.

The Stooges resented being second bananas and ventured out on their own as the Three Lost Souls. Healy replaced Larry, Curly, and Moe with three comedians whom he called the Superstooges. Healy wanted his old stooges back and threatened them with a lawsuit. When this didn't work, Healy threatened to plant a bomb in their dressing room.

The Three Stooges reluctantly returned and appeared with Healy in *The Hollywood Party*. Their act was very different from the one most people remember today. Larry was the dominant stooge and handed out most of the punishment. After *Hollywood Party* the Three Stooges went out on their own for good and appeared in over two hundred classic comedy shorts at Columbia.

RKO's *Strictly Dynamite* (1934) was Lupe's fourth and final film with Jimmy Durante. It made fun of radio, which was competing with the movies as the public's principal means of entertainment. Durante plays Moxie Slaight, an obnoxious, fast-living radio star. Lupe portrays Vera, his on-the-air foil and real-life nemesis. Ginger Rogers had been the first choice for the role but turned it down to appear in a musical with a new dancing partner, Fred Astaire.

After completing *Hollywood Party*, Lupe Velez was shocked to learn that M-G-M had not renewed her contract. The studios had decided to discontinue making films specifically for the Spanish-speaking market and Latin stars such as Lupe Velez became expendable. For the first time since she came to Hollywood, Lupe Velez was without a contract and her future as an actress was uncertain.

15

Abroad

Columbia Studio offered Lupe Velez a role in a musical, *The Girl Friend,* but she declined. She considered a $50,000 offer from a French producer but the deal fell through and she dejectedly returned to Hollywood in December 1934. The situation was taking its toll on her marriage. On January 2, 1935, Lupe filed for divorce but she and Weissmuller quickly reconciled. Lupe decided that a change of scenery might save both her career and her marriage.

In 1935, Lupe traveled to England where she was still a bankable star. Her first film abroad was a drama entitled *The Morals of Marcus.* Her costar was Ian Hunter, a versatile South African actor with an almost regal presence.

In the film, tempestuous Carlotta (Velez) is scheduled to be sold to a harem. At the last minute she stows away in the stateroom of Sir Marcus Ordeyne (Hunter). Her outrageous behavior scandalizes his proper English friends and she is whisked away to Paris by a cad named Noel Madison (Tony Pasquale), and there she makes a living performing in a cafe, after being seduced and abandoned by him. At the end of the film, Sir Charles once again comes to her rescue.

The slow-paced film was not suited to Lupe's frenetic personality. When it arrived in the United States in January 1936, *The New York Times* observed that "the new film manages to be aggressively dull when Lupe Velez is not busy exercising her fiery temper or being unconsciously amusing in her attempts to scale the proverbial dramatic heights."

Her next British movie, *Mad About Money*, was made in 1936 but not released in America until 1938. Lupe plays Carla de Huelva, an aspiring actress who passes herself off in London as a South American cattle queen. A beleaguered producer, believing she is wealthy, woos her to secure money for his new production. Silent film comedian Harry Langdon, attempting a comeback, had a small role as a tipsy theatrical angel. During the twenties Langdon's popularity rivaled that of Charlie Chaplin, Buster Keaton, and Harold Lloyd. He created a baby-like character which became almost as familiar to movie fans as Chaplin's Little Tramp. At the height of his popularity in the mid-1920s, Langdon starred in three classic comedies directed by Frank Capra: *Tramp, Tramp, Tramp, The Strong Man*, and *Long Pants*. Langdon made a fatal career move when he fired Capra and attempted to direct his own films. Like Lupe Velez, Harry Langdon went to England in the hope of reviving his career but his comeback never materialized and he died bankrupt in 1944.

Lupe Velez made only one more film in Great Britain. In 1936, she starred in a Puritanian musical comedy named *Gypsy Melody*, playing a gypsy dancer named Mila who, after overcoming her village's strict rules, marries her army-officer lover Danilo (Alfred Rode). For Lupe, *Gypsy Melody* marked the low point of her movie career.

Lupe was anxious to return to America, but before leaving England she headlined a revue, *Transatlantic Rhythm*, which after breaking in in Manchester, England opened at London's Adelphi Theatre on October 1, 1936, following a headline making backstage dispute which was duly reported in *The New York Times*: "The revue went on, all right, but only after Ruth Etting had threatened to quit because she had not been paid, after mad backstage scenes in which Lupe Velez sang a little number to quiet hollering showgirls, and after extra bobbies had been called to keep the Adelphi Theatre from being mobbed by curious Londoners who wanted to examine manifestations of American theatrical doings."

The report noted that "the theatre was a wild scene before the curtain finally rose to reveal a chorus panting from the exertions of having dressed and undressed several times while no one knew if the asbestos [curtain] would even go up. Backstage was crammed with milling crowds of the non-professionally curious, and the performers had a tough battle getting to and from their dressing rooms.

"Suddenly, up sprang Lupe Velez to save the show. Onto a chair she jumped, teetering as she pleaded with everybody to be quiet. Then she had an idea. She sang 'Ah, Sweet Mystery of Life, at Last I've Found Thee.' That did something, but not much."

The show, which also boasted the antics of American comedian Lou Holtz and the popular dance team of Buck and Bubbles, finally went on. It was produced by Jimmy Donahue, heir to the Woolworth fortune shared by his cousin, Cousin Barbara Hutton Haugwitz-Reventlow (later Mrs. Cary Grant).

"After so much extra-theatrical excitement, the show itself came as something of an anti-climax," the reviewer of *The Times of London* wrote. "It turned out to be a brilliantly hollow entertainment."

Velez befriended actress-singer Ruth Etting who said, "I've never known anyone who was sweeter to me." Etting remembered that Lupe used heat lamps to cook steaks for them between performances.

Lupe Velez came home in 1936 to perform on a vaudeville tour with husband Johnny Weissmuller for which they were paid $5,500 a week. She sang, danced, did brilliant impersonations of actresses ranging from Gloria Swanson to Katharine Hepburn, and performed in a Tarzan skit with her "Johnee."

One of Lupe's closest friends in Hollywood was Carole Lombard. As an extraordinarily beautiful child, Lombard was discovered when she was eleven years old by director Allan Dwan, who spotted her playing in the street. When she was a teenager she suffered an accident which nearly ended her promising acting career. On her way home from a dance at the Cocoanut Grove, the Bugatti her date was driving crashed and Lombard was thrown through the windshield. The accident left a long scar on her face which extended from her left cheek to the corner of her mouth. The scar was so disfiguring that Lombard refused to leave her home for months. Eventually, plastic surgery made the scar less noticeable but Lombard was always conscious of it. When she became a star, she insisted on doing her own makeup.

Carole Lombard was to become the highest paid actress of the day in Hollywood. In recognition of her stature, she was named chairperson for the 1936 Mayfair Ball which was held in the Garden Room of the Victor Hugo Restaurant in Beverly Hills. Each year the ball had a theme and Lombard proclaimed that the women dress in white. Lupe Velez, in accordance with the dress code, wore a beautiful white gown.

Nearly every big star in Hollywood was present including Humphrey Bogart, Spencer Tracy, Henry Fonda, Bing Crosby, James Stewart, Fredric March, Clark Gable, Gloria Swanson, and Barbara Stanwyck. The stellar ball was going well until Norma Shearer arrived in a strapless scarlet dress. Married to M-G-M's young genius, Irving Thalberg, Shearer had her pick of roles. Despite her unconventional looks (she was wall-eyed, a condition which left her eyes slightly askew), Norma Shearer was the undisputed Queen of Hollywood. She was the most powerful woman in Hollywood and delighted in having her own way. Shearer had a look on her face which indicated she was pleased with the disturbance she was causing.

When Lupe Velez spotted Shearer's dress she literally saw red. She considered the scarlet dress an affront to her friend Carole's honor. Lupe removed the stiletto she kept in her garter and swore, "I'm going to slit her throat." She almost succeeded before being restrained.

That night was significant for Carole Lombard in another way. She had come to the ball with Cesar Romero, a dashing young actor who was considered one of the best dancers in town. While Lombard was preoccupied with overseeing the ball, Romero proceeded to dance with other partners. Late in the evening, Clark Gable asked Lombard to dance.

Lombard and Gable had previously starred in a film, *No Man of Her Own,* and had not gotten along very well. Gable was a terrible dancer and being slightly drunk, he repeatedly stepped on Lombard's feet. Although he had come to the ball with singer Eadie Adams (not to be confused with the later Edie Adams), Clark was still married to Rhea Gable. Mrs. Gable was at the ball and fumed as her husband danced with Carole Lombard, who wore a revealing white gown which visibly aroused Gable. He asked Lombard out for a spin in his Duesenberg convertible.

That night was the beginning of the love affair between Clark Gable and Carole Lombard. Two weeks later, they were invited to a party which was being given to cheer up a friend who had suffered a nervous breakdown. Gable almost had a breakdown of his own when Lombard arrived in an ambulance and was wheeled in on a stretcher, her idea of a joke. Lombard bought a jalopy from a junkyard for $15 and gave it to Gable as a Valentine's Day present. The model T, which was painted white and covered with red hearts, came with a note which read: "You're driving me crazy." Gable was so amused by the gift that he took Lombard to the Trocadero in the $15 junker.

Less appreciated was a cockwarmer which Lombard knitted for Gable. When asked why it was so small Lombard wisecracked, "One less inch and Gable would be the Queen of Hollywood." It would be several years before Gable could secure a divorce and marry Lombard. Their marriage was one of the happiest in Hollywood until Carole Lombard's tragic death in a plane crash in 1942.

Norma Shearer survived her encounter with Lupe Velez but her reign as the Queen of Hollywood ended a year later when her husband Irving Thalberg died at age thirty-nine. She turned down the role of Scarlett O'Hara in *Gone With the Wind* because her fan club disapproved. In 1942, she married a ski instructor and retired from acting. Her last years were unhappy. She underwent shock treatment and in the 1970s attempted to throw herself out of a window of a Los Angeles skyscraper. Norma Shearer spent her last days in a single room at the Motion Picture Country Home, blind, and asking anyone who passed, "Are you Irving?"

When Lupe Velez returned to Hollywood she again became a regular at the Friday night fights. Another front row regular was none other than the Countess di Frasso. She had also returned to Hollywood after a brief stay in Italy. The Countess used to mock Lupe's ringside antics but now she herself was just as active. She became involved with some of the boxers and loudly cheered on her favorites. When they lost she sobbed openly. Lupe was unsympathetic and taunted her old rival.

Although she was approaching fifty, the Countess was still able to attract younger men. She had her own box at Santa Anita Race Track, and it was there that she met a handsome young man who attended the races every day. His name was Benjamin Siegel, but he was better known as Bugsy.

Bugsy Siegel was a career criminal and one of the founders of the infamous Murder Inc. He got his nickname as a youth when he was charged with rape. The judge told him he must have bugs in his head and the nickname stuck. Siegel hated the name and went into a murderous rage anytime someone called him Bugsy.

Despite his dapper exterior, gangster Bugsy Siegel was one of the most feared hit men. One of his victims was "Pretty" Amberg, a gangster so ugly that Ringling Brothers offered him a job as the Missing Link. Amberg liked to carve up his victims' facial features with a fork and stuff them in a laundry bag. Siegel dispatched Amberg by his favorite method of execution. He stabbed "Pretty" repeatedly in the stomach to let out the air so when he dumped the body in the river it didn't float.

Siegel was sent to California by Meyer Lansky to take control of organized crime's gambling and prostitution empires on the West Coast. Once established, Siegel moved in on the Film Extras Guild and devised a shakedown operation which threatened to shut down film production in Hollywood unless he received payoffs.

The Countess fell madly in love with Bugsy Siegel and provided his entry into Hollywood society. Hedda Hopper wrote: "Dorothy di Frasso conned some of the biggest names in our town to take this hoodlum into their homes." Siegel rented opera singer Lawrence Tibbett's mansion* and threw lavish, $5,000 a night parties. He socialized with movie stars, most notably his boyhood pal George Raft, Jean Harlow, Gary Cooper, Cary Grant, and Clark Gable. Reportedly, he blackmailed some of the stars by threatening to expose their past indiscretions.

---

*James Toback took liberties in his screenplay to the 1991 film *Bugsy* by having Siegel buy the house on threat of violence.

Bugsy was extremely vain about his appearance. Every day he meticulously rubbed cream on his face and wore an elastic chinstrap to keep his handsome face from sagging. Siegel had a morbid fear of going bald was in constant denial about his obviously thinning hair. His barbers, fearful of violence, assured him that there were imaginary new hairs growing on his scalp. Siegel was envious of the full head of hair of his bodyguard, Mack "Killer" Gray. One night, he offered Gray $2,500 if he could cut off his hair. He threw the clippings into a fireplace and cast a spell as if he were a witch doctor. To his chagrin, his hair continued to fall out while Gray's hair grew in even thicker.

Despite her wealth, the Countess di Frasso was always getting involved in get-richer-quick schemes. In 1937, she and Bugsy embarked on an ill-fated search for buried treasure. They met a Canadian fortune hunter in a bar. He spun a tale about a nineteenth century British sea captain who had buried $300 million in gold on uninhabited Cocos Island near Costa Rica. The treasure represented the national treasury of Peru which had been in the midst of a revolution. The prospector drew a treasure map on the tablecloth with the Countess' lipstick. He promised to locate the gold if the Countess financed the expedition.

The Countess chartered a three-mastered schooner, the Metha Nelson, while Bugsy rounded up a cutthroat crew of modern day pirates. Most of the twenty man crew was recruited from bookie joints and only three had any sailing experience. The Countess always traveled in style and stocked the ship with expensive caviar and the finest wines. Siegel expressed the sentiments of the crew when he exclaimed, "We're going to grab the stuff and beat it. And then we're going to go home rich."

They soon discovered the reason that Cocos Island had remained uninhabited. The island was an insect infested bog which reeked with the stench of animal feces. For ten days they searched every inch of the island and blew half of it away with explosives but found not an ounce of gold. Half mad, Bugsy Siegel, nattily dressed in an impeccably tailored pinstripe suit and pointed two-tone shoes, lobbed hand grenades into the jungle in frustration.

The angry crew was near mutiny on the return trip. To make matters worse the ship's engines broke down and the Metha Nelson floated aimlessly for three days. A typhoon was approaching in the Gulf of Tehuan- tepec but the ship was rescued at the last minute by a passing tramp steamer which towed it to Acapulco. Thus ended the voyage of the Metha Nelson, known thereafter as the "Ship From Hell."

The Metha Nelson fiasco did not discourage the Countess di Frasso and Bugsy Siegel from launching another dubious moneymaking scheme. Two wacky scientists approached the Countess with a new super explosive which they called atomite. They demon- strated the awesome power of the new explosive by blowing away part of a mountain in the Imperial Valley Desert. After observing the explosion Bugsy Siegel said wistfully, "If I'd only had some of this stuff in the old days."

The Countess bought the rights to the new weapon for $50,000. She notified Italian dictator Benito Mus- solini who paid a $40,000 downpayment for a demon- stration. When the atomite turned out to be a dud, Il

Duce was furious and threatened to throw the Countess and Bugsy in prison unless they returned the
$40,000 immediately. He seized the Villa Madama, the
Countess' palatial estate, and made her and Bugsy
endure the humiliation of staying in the stable. The
Villa Madama became Mussolini's guest home where
he hosted visiting heads of state.

During his stay in Italy, Bugsy Siegel was introduced
to Nazi leaders Hermann Goering and Joseph Goebbels. Siegel hated Nazis and vowed, "I'm going to kill
that fat bastard [Goering] and that dirty Goebbels too!"
The course of world history and our perception of
Bugsy Siegel may have been changed if the Countess
hadn't stopped him.

Bugsy didn't care much for European high society.
Referring to the Villa Madama he said, "This joint was
bigger than Grand Central Station, and half the guys
she had hanging around were counts or dukes or kings
out of a job." One thing which did impress him was the
painting of Raphael. Bugsy said, "That Ralphie [Raph-
ael], you'd never know he painted them hundreds of
years ago. They were like they were just painted."

The Countess di Frasso was embarrassed by Bugsy's
hoodlum reputation and introduced him to her society
friends as Bart Siegel, hoping that he'd be mistaken for
a baronet. She introduced him to Italy's exiled King
Umberto II who told the Countess, "He acted rather
oddly for a baron. He tried to sell me dynamite." When
he learned that Siegel was a notorious gangster, the
King was outraged that the United States tolerated
such behavior. The Countess gently reminded him
that Italy was the birthplace of organized crime.

Eventually, Bugsy Siegel dumped the Countess di

Frasso for younger, even bustier women such as Marie "The Body" McDonald and Virginia Hill. Siegel helped establish Las Vegas as a gambling mecca when he built the Flamingo Hotel and Casino. In 1947, the forty-one-year-old Bugsy Siegel was murdered in a gangland slaying while sitting in the living room of Virginia Hill's Beverly Hills mansion. One of the assassin's bullets blew one of Bugsy's celebrated blue eyes across the room. Only five family members attended his funeral. The Countess di Frasso declined comment on his death.

During World War II, the FBI suspected the Countess di Frasso of being an Axis spy because of her connections to Mussolini. They kept her under constant surveillance but could never prove their suspicions. The Countess, well into her fifties, was reduced to cruising down Hollywood Boulevard in a chauffeured limousine, picking up young men and hustlers. She frequented wild Hollywood parties which featured sadomasochistic sex. On January 1, 1954, the Countess di Frasso died on a train traveling between New York and her beloved Hollywood.

16

The Tailwaggers Ball

Lupe Velez's first movie upon her return to Hollywood was RKO's *High Flyers* (1937). The film was directed by Eddie Cline, the director of *Million Dollar Legs*, who was known for his manic comedy style. She costarred with the zany team of Bert Wheeler and Robert Woolsey. Broadway headliners before getting into movies in *Rio Rita* in 1929, Wheeler and Woolsey made twenty-three films together but this was to be their last.

Also appearing in the film was Margaret Dumont, best remembered as the matronly socialite in seven Marx Brothers films. Dumont began her career as a showgirl and was trained as an opera singer. She boasted, "I'm the best straight woman in Hollywood." Marjorie Lord, Jack Carson, and Paul Harvey were in the cast as well.

High Flyers was a slapstick comedy with Wheeler and Woolsey playing numbskulls tricked into smuggling gems into the country. Much of the action takes place at the mansion of Margaret Dumont. Lupe Velez has little to do in her role as Juanita Morales, other than perform a mundane poolside number called "Keep Your Head Above the Water." The production was marred by the serious illness of Robert Woolsey, who suffered from a terminal kidney ailment and died a year after the completion of the film.

Lupe Velez decided to try her luck at radio. She performed on the CBS program "Under Two Flags" and was reunited with director Cecil B. De Mille. Other stars appearing on the program were Olivia De Havilland, Herbert Marshall, and Lionel Atwill. By all accounts, Lupe stole the show.

Lionel Atwill was the personification of Dr. Jekyll and Mr. Hyde. On the surface he gave the impression of being a cultured English gentleman. He owned an impressive collection of Old Masters' paintings and bought one after each film he completed. Atwill made his reputations playing mad scientists in films such as Doctor X. His favorite pastime was attending murder trials. He believed all women had a secret desire to be dominated and said, "Women love the men they fear." Atwill had the peculiar habit of sleeping with his pet python, Elsie, and had a talking macaw named Copulate. He staged Bacchanalian orgies at his home on d'Este Drive and his film career was destroyed when scandalous details about one of his wild Christmas parties were made public.

The pickings had become increasingly slim in Hollywood for Lupe and late 1937 she returned to Mexico. It was the first time she'd been home in eleven years and she was overwhelmed by the reception which awaited her. She was a national hero in Mexico and a crowd of ten thousand pushed one another just to catch a glimpse of her. Lupe was afraid she was going to be torn to pieces by her fans and confessed she was "enchanted but scared to death."

Her first Mexican movie, *La Zandunga*, was a musical comedy about the relationship between Lupe Velez (as herself) and her sailor lover, Juancho, played by Mexican leading man, Arturo de Cordova. De Cordova was a handsome actor who later gained minor fame in Hollywood in the forties. He and Lupe began a torrid love affair and she admitted she was heartbroken when the relationship ended.

The film premiered in New York in March 1938, and received good reviews. *The Times* wrote: "Lupe's acting, particularly when she is trying to veil her sorrows with assumed light-heartedness at the wedding fiesta of her friend, is first rate." Lupe was offered a four-picture contract in Mexico at the attractive salary of $4,500 per week, and seriously considered the offer. But she wanted to return to Hollywood to reestablish herself in America. Besides, her marriage to Johnny Weissmuller was on the rocks.

Lupe and her "Johnee" continually argued, often so loudly that their shouts could be heard throughout the neighborhood. An interested listener was onetime actress turned gossip columnist Hedda Hopper who lived across the street from the Weissmullers.

Born Edna Furry in Altoona, Pennsylvania on June 2, 1890, she was the daughter of a butcher. She married De Wolf Hopper, a vaudeville star old enough to be her father, and a strange looking man with blueish skin, the result of swallowing silver nitrate.

After an unhappy marriage, she divorced Hopper

and came to Hollywood where she began a career as an actress. She fabricated her background to make it sound more glamorous than it really was. She hated the name Edna and paid an astrologer $10 to give her a new name, Hedda. Hopper was fifty years old when she became as a gossip columnist in 1937. She began modestly by writing a weekly newsletter about Hollywood in the *Washington Times-Herald,* but her column became so popular that it was nationally syndicated a year later. Her principal rival, Louella Parsons, had made a lot of enemies and many stars got their revenge by giving Hedda Hopper their scoops.

Hedda quickly made enemies of her own. Joseph Cotten kicked her in the rear after she linked him romantically with Deanna Durbin. Ann Sheridan showed her displeasure by dumping mashed potatoes in Hedda's lap. Joan Bennett sent her a skunk as a Valentine's Day gift. Most stars gave her expensive presents in order to stay in her good graces. Her trademark was her fabulous hats; she bought one hundred-fifty a year. It was rumored that Hopper, who disliked men after her bad marriage, promoted the careers of young actors who slept with her.

Fortunately for Lupe, because of her openness about her personal life, she was a favorite of Hedda's and gave her plenty to write about. It was evident that Lupe's marriage to Johnny Weissmuller was coming to an end. She began being seen in public with other men, most notably actor Bruce Cabot and producer Eddie Mannix.

Bruce Cabot was born Etienne Pelissier de Bujac in 1904. The square jaw actor, who starred in numerous films including *King Kong,* was a hard-drinker and close buddy of another carouser, Errol Flynn. Their friendship ended when Cabot sued Flynn after his production company backed out of a deal with him.

Eddie Mannix, a longtime executive at M-G-M and one of the most powerful men in Hollywood, was a former bouncer at Palisades Park in Fort Lee, New Jersey, just across the river from New York City. Mannix was a tough, macho man who was once described as looking like "a boxer with a cauliflower ear for a face." His nickname was "Chinaman" because of his slanting eyes. In spite of his tough image, Eddie Mannix was respected by movie executives and actors alike.

One of Lupe's last public appearances with Johnny Weissmuller was at the Tailwaggers Ball held at the Hollywood Hotel. The purpose of the Ball, organized by Bette Davis, was to raise money for an animal hospital and to train seeing-eye dogs for the blind. Many of Hollywood's biggest stars attended including James Stewart, Errol Flynn, Norma Shearer, and Joel McCrea.

An unexpected guest arrived while the stars were playing a game of musical chairs. Howard Hughes walked in the ballroom, dressed in a rumpled tuxedo. Hughes was not known as an animal lover and everyone wondered why he came. Soon his intentions became apparent.

Hughes ambled over to Bette Davis who was dressed in a gorgeous low-cut pink lace gown. Davis was the hottest actress in Hollywood, having just won the first of two consecutive Academy Awards for best actress. Hughes apologized for being late, "I'm sorry I missed dinner. I've been working on a plane for the government."

Bette Davis took his arm and led him to the kitchen where she ordered a four-course meal. He responded to her kindness by purchasing dozens of raffle tickets to benefit the charity. Almost immediately, she fell in love with him. "He was so debonair and handsome," she remembered. She responded to his shy, self-conscious nature which brought out her maternal instincts. During the evening Hughes seemed mesmerized by Davis' cleavage and sneaked a peek whenever he could.

Only one obstacle stood in the way of their relationship. Bette Davis was married to bandleader Ham Nelson. Bette Davis and Howard Hughes began to see each other secretly. She wanted to make love and couldn't understand why a man with Hughes' playboy reputation had not made sexual advances.

Davis was shocked when Hughes confessed that their love could never be consummated. He admitted that he suffered from recurrent ejaculatory impotence which resulted from a recently ended affair with Katharine Hepburn. Hughes claimed that due to the break-up of the much-publicized relationship, he suffered from low self-esteem and diminished sexual performance.

Bette Davis considered Katharine Hepburn to be her main acting rival in Hollywood. Davis hated her own appearance and thought Hepburn's face was perfect. She was determined to cure Hughes' sexual problem and gradually he responded to her tender care. She found Hughes to be an expert lover, well-endowed but reluctant to show his true feelings. Hughes expressed his gratitude by making love to her on a bed covered with gardenias, her favorite flower.

Ham Nelson learned about the affair and conceived a plan which could ruin both his wife and Howard Hughes. With the help of a private detective, Nelson bugged the couple's Coldwater Canyon home. He kept the building under round-the-clock surveillance from a sound truck parked on a side street near the house. One night he was listening to their lovemaking and experienced the rage of a cuckolded husband. Nelson rushed into the bedroom and caught Davis and Hughes in the middle of sex. Bette Davis screamed hysterically as Howard Hughes threw a wild punch at Nelson which missed.

Ham Nelson revealed his conditions for blackmail. Unless Howard Hughes paid him $70,000 he would make the tape public. He threatened not only to expose Hughes as an adulterer but to reveal his impotence. The consequences were even more devastating for Bette Davis. The resulting sex scandal would almost certainly destroy her career.

The millionaire followed the instructions and sent Nelson a check for $70,000. Hughes, fearful of another blackmail attempt, ended the relationship with Bette Davis. He also decided it might be necessary to silence Ham Nelson forever and contacted a professional killer about the possibility of murdering the blackmailer. Somehow Ham Nelson learned of the plan and Hughes abandoned the idea of killing him.

Ham Nelson filed for divorce, citing irreconcilable differences but making no mention of adultery. As a matter of honor, Bette Davis borrowed money from the studio to repay Howard Hughes. Although he was one of the richest men in the world, Hughes accepted the money. The next year, on the anniversary of the repayment, Howard Hughes sent Bette Davis a single flower to commemorate the event. It was the most expensive flower she would ever receive.

Like Bette Davis, Lupe Velez's marriage was about to end. She and Johnny Weissmuller decided to spend an evening at a night spot on the Sunset Strip named Ciro's. The nightclub had previously been the Club Seville, notable for its glass dance floor which overlooked a pool stocked with carp. The club failed when women complained that they felt uneasy about fish looking up their dresses. Ciro's installed a conventional dance floor and became one of the most successful nightclubs in Hollywood.

Lupe and Johnny argued all evening, which was not unusual. She was always throwing fits in public and he usually was able to restrain himself. The strain of the marriage finally took its toll on his patience. Without warning, Johnny Weissmuller grabbed his salad and dumped it on Lupe's head. For once, Lupe Velez was speechless.

In early 1938, Lupe filed for divorce, claiming physical and mental cruelty. She described Johnny Weissmuller as a "furniture breaking caveman." During the proceedings Lupe charged that "Johnee" was so cheap that he wouldn't even give her the money to go to a beauty parlor. Judge Charles Burnett replied, "He probably thought you didn't need the beauty treatment." The divorce was granted and Weissmuller was ordered to pay Lupe $200 a week alimony for three years. Lupe Velez received the Beverly Hills mansion while Johnny Weissmuller was given the speedboat and the schooner.

Weissmuller continued to star in Tarzan movies and later in a series of Jungle Jim films. Hopelessly typecast in Tarzan-like roles and limited as an actor, he retired from the screen. In 1959, Weissmuller was playing in a celebrity golf tournament in Cuba. The revolution was in progress and rebel guerrillas surrounded the golf course. It became apparent that they planned to kidnap the Americans. Weissmuller rose to his feet, beat his chest, and let out his famous Tarzan yell. The soldiers recognized Weissmuller and escorted him to safety.

In his later years, Weissmuller was the proprietor of a health food store. His personal life continued to be unsettled and he was married six times. He died in 1984 at age eighty.

Lupe Velez denied she was to blame for the divorce. "Because I am supposed to be nuts everyone blames me entirely for the divorce. In some of my movies I am crazy, sure. That's all right for my work, but offstage I am not temperamental. I am very easy to get along with, yes?" Nobody dared to contradict her.

She explained in a magazine article how the press had distorted her relationship with Johnny Weissmuller.

"I'll tell you right now that I was not to blame for what happened. You know what? I love newspaper men, the press, but some of them have been very mean to me. Like the time Johnny and I were flying east. I had taken a pill to help me sleep. Johnny won't take them, but anyway, I was sleeping in my chair—they didn't have berths then—when a book from the rack above fell down and hit me right on the eye. Of course, it got black and I felt awful because I know right away what the press will say. So I got a paper for what do you call it, testimonies. I went among the other passengers asking them to sign saying that a book hit me, not Johnny. But what do the headlines say later on? That's right. 'JOHNNY SOCKS LUPE!'

"Then another time, Johnny and I were on a plane going to the coast. Johnny was plane sick—oh! He was green sick! He said, 'Mommy, I'm dying!' I said, 'All right, sweetheart. I'll take care of you.' So we arrived. Instead of going to the airport bus I told the porter to put the bags in a cab that was standing there. I had the bags and Johnny all in when a man came up with the driver and said that he had ordered the car and that this was his regular driver. So I started to haul out the bags—Johnny was still groaning inside the cab. Just then two men with cameras came up and snap, there I was with a bag in my hand and Johnny stretched out in the taxi. What do you think the headlines were this time? I'll tell you—'LUPE LEAVES JOHNNY AT AIRPORT!' "

Lupe bought the thirteen room mansion which Jack Dempsey had built for Estelle Taylor in Senseneda, Baja, California. Not one to mull over her divorce, she was soon telephoning gossip columnists to give them juicy details of her new love affairs.

One of her favorite escorts following the divorce was British leading man, Henry Wilcoxon, who had starred in numerous films including *Cleopatra* and *The Last of the Mohicans* and was a cohort of Cecil B. De Mille. Like most of Lupe's boyfriends, Wilcoxon was strong and handsome, an excellent horseman and swordsman as well as a talented designer and artist. De Mille described Wilcoxon as "a man of many talents." Lupe

Velez and Henry Wilcoxon were often seen out dancing. One photograph published in *Silver Screen* magazine showed Lupe leading a Conga line with the caption: "Dancers always love life."

Once the divorce was over, the hostility between Lupe Velez and Johnny Weissmuller subsided. When asked to name the ten most interesting men she ever met, Johnny Weissmuller headed the list. Others named on the list were Clark Gable, her old enemy Jack Dempsey, President Franklin Roosevelt, Ernest Hemingway, George S. Kaufman, Ed Wynn, Lawrence Tibbett, composer George Enesco, and labor leader John L. Lewis.

Gary Cooper's name was conspicuously absent.

17

The Black Widow

Lupe Velez hoped that a return to the stage might revitalize her career in America. She was offered a starring role in James Caan's play, "7-11," but the production was shelved before it reached Broadway. Luckily the Shubert Brothers signed her to star in their new musical, *You Never Know*, along with Clifton Webb and torch singer Libby Holman.

You Never Know was Cole Porter's musical adaptation of a romantic comedy, *By Candlelight*, which had played on Broadway in 1929. Born into an incredibly wealthy family in Indiana, Porter graduated from Yale and briefly attended the Harvard Law School. After a short stint in the French Foreign Legion, he returned to the United States where he began his remarkable songwriting career. Porter was a homosexual and, despite his sexual preference, married a beautiful and wealthy lady.

In 1937, Porter began work on *You Never Know*. On October 24, he was horseback riding when his mount shied away from a clump of bushes. The horse reared and fell on its side, crushing Porter's leg. Before Porter was able to free himself, the horse rolled over, injuring his other leg. Although he suffered fractures of both legs, Porter claimed that he wrote the lyrics to "At Long Last Love," one of the songs featured in *You Never Know,* while he was waiting for the ambulance.

Porter was hospitalized for months as doctors tried to save his leg, which was reset seven times. "There are at least a thousand little men in these legs and they're all carrying sharp knives. They're jabbing all over," Porter said, describing his constant, unbearable pain. The pain was so intense that he took over a dozen different sedatives to relieve his agony. As a result of the accident, Cole Porter became a semi-invalid. He had difficulty walking and a burly attendant would sometimes throw him over his shoulder like a sack of potatoes and carry him from place to place. Porter received shock treatments to help him cope with the pain and the psychological damage he suffered. Eventually, he underwent thirty-five operations and years later doctors were forced to amputate his leg.

While hospitalized, Cole Porter continued to write the music for *You Never Know.* To celebrate his release from the hospital, a gala surprise party was thrown at the Perroquet Suite of the Waldorf-Astoria in New York. Among the guests were the Countess di Frasso, Richard Rodgers, and Clifton Webb. Porter reassured Webb that the score for the show would be completed on time.

Since Porter was unable to go to the theater for rehearsals, the Shubert Brothers sent the entire cast and musicians to Porter's fabulous suite at the Waldorf

Towers. Lupe Velez and the rest of the cast performed the show from start to finish under Porter's watchful eye. Cole Porter was wildly enthusiastic and commented that he thought *You Never Know* was the best score he had ever written. Later he completely changed his mind and said, "It was the worst show with which I was ever connected."

It premiered in New Haven in March 1938, with a pre-Broadway tour scheduled for Boston, Washington, Philadelphia, Pittsburgh, Detroit, Chicago, Des Moines, Indianapolis, Columbus, Buffalo, and Hartford, before a fall opening in New York. The initial reception for the show was encouraging. The opening night crowd in New Haven was the largest for a play since pre-Depression days and, a week later in Boston, Mrs. Calvin Coolidge, widow of the President, came out of seclusion to see the show.

Despite its initial success, it soon became apparent that the show was in trouble. Show doctor George Abbott was brought in to try to save the production. Cole Porter lamented that the show had been rewritten so often that he compared it to being married to the wrong woman seven times. While *You Never Know* was not vintage Cole Porter, it may have succeeded were it not for the bickering of the cast. From the outset the rest of the cast was overshadowed by the outrageous behavior of Lupe Velez.

The only member of the cast she seemed to get along with was Clifton Webb. Born Webb Parmelee Hollenbech on November 19, 1889, he was an opera singer before he became one of the leading actors on Broadway. Webb was a homosexual and his dominant mother, Mabelle, who served as his agent and confidante, was rarely out of sight. He was known for his snooty demeanor and wry sense of humor. Once he was invited to a dinner party by Tallulah Bankhead, who was furious when he told her he was bringing along a Japanese trapeze artist as his date. The date turned out to be Greta Garbo, making a rare public appearance.

Lupe Velez and Libby Holman took an instant dislike to one another. Holman was unhappy that Cole Porter had written songs especially for Lupe Velez but not for her, and was angered because Lupe frequently upstaged her. In New Haven, the feuding women came to blows during a curtain call. Holman was half a foot taller than Velez, but the match was no contest. Libby emerged from the fracas with a black eye.

Not satisfied with the outcome, Lupe threatened to kill Libby Holman. The stage manager took the threats seriously and every night escorted Holman from her dressing room to the stage. Libby Holman was so nearsighted that she felt her way around the stage and occasionally tripped over the scenery. Lupe devised an ingenious plan to rid herself of Libby Holman. She urinated in the wings, hoping that the myopic Holman would slip and break her neck. She was disappointed when this never happened. The turmoil was too much for Cole Porter who had a breakdown and spent the summer recuperating in Europe.

Lupe Velez couldn't have picked a worse enemy. Libby Holman had a notorious past. One member of the cast recalled, "She reminded me of a black widow spider." Elisabeth Holman was born in Cincinnati in 1904, the daughter of noted attorney, Alfred Holman. Rebellious even as a youth, she was arrested for nude sunbathing in Deauville, France. Once, when she was pulled over for speeding the policeman said, "I'm going to have to pinch you."

"I'd rather be tickled," Libby replied.

She attended the University of Cincinnati, where she established a reputation as a femme fatale. Later, she enrolled in Columbia Law School but dropped out to pursue a career in show business.

Libby Holman's first role was a streetwalker in the road company of *The Fool*, a play based on the life of St. Francis of Assisi.

In 1925, she made her New York debut as one of the Theatre Guild Junior Players in a Rodgers and Hart revue *The Garrick Gaieties*. Holman had got the $30 a week part because the producer had noticed her beautiful legs. She had a mischievous sense of humor which she displayed during the show. Fellow performer Sterling Holloway had to sing a line which went, "I sit and sigh." Just before the line Libby whispered, "shit," in Holloway's ear. As expected, the power of suggestion caused him to sing, "I shit and sigh." Richard Rodgers, in the orchestra pit, ducked his head out of sight in embarrassment as the audience roared with laughter.

In 1929, Libby Holman costarred with Clifton Webb and Fred Allen in *The Little Show*. The highlight of which was Libby's sultry rendition of "Moanin' Low." Her sensuous contralto voice was described by *New York Times'* critic Brooks Atkinson as a "deep purple flame." Playwright Tennessee Williams wrote: "Her voice was the sound of a siren in heat." One admirer observed, "Libby's voice was so compelling that she made the entire theater sweat." Her performance was so captivating that once, after twelve curtain calls, the composer, Howard Dietz, had to beg the audience to let Libby go home.

The same cast returned the following season for "Three's a Crowd." Wearing a low-cut black gown, Libby caused a sensation with her provocative rendition of "Body and Soul," a song considered so sexy radio stations around the country banned it. At age twenty-four, Holman was acclaimed as New York's premier torch singer. Columnist Walter Winchell dubbed her "The Statue of Libby."

Libby was uncomfortable singing one of the show's songs, "Something to Remember You By." She decided she needed someone to sing to and selected a young saxophonist with the California Collegians to stand with his back to the audience. The young man was Fred MacMurray and he soon made his name in Hollywood.

Holman attributed her distinctive voice to a botch tonsillectomy she had as a youth. By mistake, the doctor removed an extra piece of her throat which gave her voice a prolonged vibralto and added fullness to the low notes. Libby preserved her tonsils in alcohol and carried them in a jar wherever she went.

Libby Holman was called the sexiest woman in America. Raven haired and sloe-eyed, Libby had an attractive face, Cupid's bow lips, and a sleek body that attracted both men and women. She loved to display her long, slender, perpetually tan legs and was especially proud of her breasts. Holman never wore a bra and took intramuscular shots to keep her breasts firm. Her nickname was "T.P." which stood for "tit proud," and she often wore no clothes in her dressing room. Louise Brooks, the great screen beauty, once saw Holman nude and described her body as "like one of those exquisite bronze figurines that rise from Roman fountains."

Libby's myopia once caused her to fall into a man-hole in New York and, on another occasion, she managed to trip over a cow. She slid her feet on the stage so she wouldn't trip over anything. The audience, unaware of her nearsightedness, marveled at her sexy "serpent" walk. When she squinted, her expression was interpreted as a come-hither look.

Holman knew full well her sex appeal. "While a girl is young and voluptuous, she can't help but be adored," she said. Libby preferred androgynous, almost pretty men, especially those who confided their sexual inadequacies to her. Each night she would make five or six dates, then select one at the last minute.

Holman made no attempt to hide her own bisexuality. "I love men in bed but I really love women," she confessed. One of her lovers was Tallulah Bankhead; she delighted in dressing in a man's suit and lunching with Tallulah and Bea Lillie. Her longest love affair was with Louisa Carpenter, the du Pont heiress. Carpenter, a tall, beautiful strawberry blonde with a milky, white complexion, dressed like a man, walked like a man, and talked like a man. She also was a crack shot and a noted aviatrix. She invited Libby aboard her 137 foot yacht, the Galaxy, and seduced her by stripping to the waist. To show her gratitude, Louise bought Libby a sixteen-cylinder Rolls-Royce convertible.

Libby had some strange ideas about sex. She believed people should have their sexual organs in their throat because, in her words, "so people could start screwing right away." After her show was over on-Broadway, Holman invariably went uptown to Harlem, where the night life was totally uninhibited. Her tourguide through Harlem was a small, black hunchback known as "Monkey." Libby frequented the "sex circus" where drag parades and sex orgies were commonplace.

Libby Holman was pursued by many men, especially Zachary Smith Reynolds, the twenty-year-old heir to the $100 million Reynolds tobacco fortune. A stage-door Johnny, he became obsessed with Libby and attended every performance of *Three's a Crowd*. Libby resisted his advances and Reynolds threatened suicide if she didn't marry him. "I'll die if I can't have you," he told her, and he meant it.

Reynolds carried a loaded Mauser with him at all times, claiming that he was terrified of being kidnapped. At night he placed a dummy under the covers and slept under his bed, covered by newspapers. He was insanely jealous of Holman's relationship with Louisa Carpenter, and once drove his car into the ocean after discovering Libby with her.

Reynolds was also a world-class aviator and broke the transcontinental flying record from New York to Los Angeles by six hours. When Libby informed him that she was going on an around-the-world cruise with Louisa Carpenter, Reynolds threatened to crash his plane into the ocean. Finally, his persistence paid off, and he and Libby Holman were married on November 29, 1931.

He brought his new bride to Reynolda, the family's incredible thousand-acre estate in Winston-Salem, North Carolina. The sixty room mansion had its own private golf course and a spring-fed swimming pool. The Reynolds family were treated like royalty in the region.

The marriage was stormy from the start. The two argued violently and followed their quarrels with intense lovemaking. The union ended tragically following a Fourth of July barbecue at Reynolda in 1932 with a few close friends. One hundred proof corn liquor was served and Libby challenged a guest to a drinking contest of her specially prepared "divebombers."

After prevailing, the intoxicated Holman disrobed in front of the guests, which enraged her husband. She staggered off to the east wing of the house where a guest reported seeing her in bed with her husband's best friend, Ab Walker. Guests were startled by the sound of a gunshot. Libby Holman, dressed in a blood-splattered, peach-colored, silk negligee, stumbled into the room and said, "Smith's shot himself," before collapsing on the divan.

The coroner's inquest was held four days later in Libby's bedroom, and she made a spectacular entrance, wearing a diaphanous nightgown. There were inconsistencies in Holman and Walker's stories and it was determined that the fatal shot was fired at least eighteen inches from Reynolds' head, an unusual distance for a suicide victim.

Libby Holman and Ab Walker were charged with first degree murder. Libby's father, Alfred Holman, was summoned to defend his daughter. The sensational murder case was proclaimed the "trial of the century" and was front page news across the country. The *New York Daily Mirror* planned a twenty-seven part series on the trial and described Libby Holman as a "sensuous sex pirate with the primitive emotions of a jungle girl."

Libby disappeared after the inquest and resurfaced

shortly before the trial was to begin. She entered the courthouse dressed in a black veil which totally obscured her face, and the press immediately labeled her as the "black widow." A startling revelation occurred when it was learned that Libby was pregnant with Smith Reynolds' child. During the proceedings, Libby knitted baby clothes.

Holman told the police that her husband, who had often threatened to commit suicide, stood in front of her and calmly blew his brains out. Privately, however, she admitted, "I was so drunk I don't know if I shot him or not." Her brilliant defense was to bring out embarrassing revelations about Smith Reynolds, hoping the the Reynolds family would not prosecute. The strategy worked perfectly and the family used their influence to get the charges dropped.

Libby Holman received a $750,000 settlement, with an additional $6.6 million placed in a trust for her son, Christopher. She considered returning to the stage. Ironically, during her marriage, she had been offered the lead in a play, *Periphery*, which was about a woman and her lover who murder a man and then try to make it appear to be an accident. In 1933, she made a brief comeback in a musical called *Revenge With Music*.

Libby Holman went into seclusion for five years. In 1937, she built a sixteen-room-estate in Connecticut which she named Treetops, but the dining room of Treetops was a replica of the Governor's mansion in Williamsburg. The bathrooms were furnished with white mink throw rugs, mirrored bathtubs, solid gold fixtures, and dolphin shaped spouts. Over a million daffodils were planted on the grounds and a pure white daffodil was named Libby Holman in her honor.

Libby Holman was coaxed out of retirement by her old friend, Clifton Webb, to appear in *You Never Know*. The long-awaited return of the woman known as the "Wicked Lady of Broadway" was the talk of New York. Actress Patsy Kelly asked Tallulah Bankhead, "Is Libby working again?" Tallulah answered, "Yes, darling. She's in between murders."

Libby Holman's feud with Lupe Velez overshadowed *You Never Know*, which opened at the Winter Garden Theater in New York on September 21, 1938. The plot concerned a baron who decides to exchange identities with his butler, Gaston (Clifton Webb), in order to court an aristocrat (Holman). A comedy of errors develops when her maid, Maria (Velez), impersonates her mistress. Lupe Velez sang, "You Never Know" and "What Shall I Do?" and performed "From Alpha to Omega" in duet with Clifton Webb, and also delighted audiences with her uncanny imitations of Shirley Temple and Katharine Hepburn.

For the most part, the reviews were not enthusiastic. John Mason Brown of the *New York Post* noted: "You might think that with Cole Porter on hand to supply music and lyrics for such performers as Webb, Velez, and Holman, the results would be sprightly, but in spite of what you may have thought, permit me to report that you are wrong." Brown described Libby Holman as the "Lady Macbeth of Jazz."

As for Lupe, she didn't fare any better. *Vogue* magazine wrote: "Lupe Velez had no more dignity than a donkey." Brooks Atkinson of *The New York Times* was slightly kinder, describing her manic performance as "a strange collection of some things that are funny and a great many more that are only perpetual motion."

The crew called the encounter between Velez and Holman, the Mexican Spitfire vs. the Jewish Witch. Lupe, agitated by Libby Holman, was on her worst behavior. She screamed at the stage manager, and director, Rowland Leigh, walked out, vowing not to return until the women settled their differences.

Libby also displayed contempt for cast and crew. She was known to write notes to herself addressed, "My Divine Libby," and signed, "I love you, divine Libby, wonderful Libby, beautiful Libby." Holman smoked big Havana cigars, ate raw meat, and wore bright japonica colored fingernail polish. She practically bathed in Jungle Gardenia perfume and its scent pervaded everything she touched. Lupe Velez countered by carrying a huge bottle of Chanel.

The situation between Lupe and Libby continued to deteriorate. Libby, who owned a huge Great Dane named X-Ray, despised the six yappy Chihuahuas Lupe kept with her at all times. Libby thought Lupe was a vulgar, Mexican peasant and told her so.

"Libby, you bastard. You son-of-a-bitch. I kill you with this," Lupe screamed, flashing a large diamond ring which Johnny Weissmuller had bought for her.

Libby responded by taunting her with an equally large rhinestone ring which she claimed resembled Lupe Velez's nose. She told Clifton Webb, "You've got to give her credit. Lupe aspired and succeeded in becoming little more than a cheap whore."

Clifton Webb, who was the only person who got along with both women, tried to act as peacemaker. When he realized that Lupe Velez was serious about killing Libby Holman, he took her aside. Lupe showed him her ring and said, "This is the ring I'm going to murder that Jewish bitch with." After each outburst, Lupe fell to her knees, crossed herself, and prayed for forgiveness.

Webb attempted to calm her down. "Lupe, you must not say such things. One day you'll turn them all against yourself." At the time neither Clifton Webb nor Lupe Velez could realize how prophetic his warning would be.

Financial problems caused some of the members of the cast and crew to accept pay cuts. In order to save overtime, Lee and J. J. Shubert, the producers, instructed stagehands to remove props and scenery while the show was still in progress. By the end of the show, the stage was nearly bare. *You Never Know* closed after only seventy-eight performances. Many critics felt that its failure marked the end of the career of Cole Porter. He soon proved them wrong.

Libby Holman's hatred of Lupe Velez never diminished. She told Clifton Webb that she had never disliked a person as much as she disliked Lupe Velez. For years, Holman had believed she was a witch. She owned a black fan which she called the "Witch's fan." She was convinced that she possessed sorceress' powers and sometimes signed letters, "The Witch." One of her strangest beliefs was that she was a conduit, a medium from which death radiated to others. She told aviatrix Louisa Carpenter, one of her many (male and female) lovers, "I used to be a black witch. Now I'm a white one."

Clifton Webb laughed, "You'll turn into a witch yet, my dear." Libby responded by putting a hex on Lupe Velez.

The year after *You Never Know* closed, Libby Hol-

man married Ralph Holmes, a handsome actor, twelve
years her junior. During World War II, while Holmes
served in the Royal Canadian Air Force, Libby admitted many infidelities. When he came home from the
war, Libby expelled him from Treetops. Shortly thereafter, Holmes' body was found in his New York apartment. The coroner ruled that he died from an overdose
of sleeping pills.

The one person Libby Holman truly loved was her
son, Christopher. She employed seven bodyguards to
protect him from kidnapping. For his sixth birthday
party she hired Benny Goodman, Gene Krupa, Lionel
Hampton, and Billie Holiday to perform. "It was a hell
of a party," Libby said, in an understatement.

Her life, already filled with death, was shattered
when her seventeen-year-old son was killed attempting
to climb California's Mt. Whitney. Although she inherited the $7 million which had been placed in her son's
trust, Libby Holman became obsessed with death. She
covered the walls of her home with photographs of her
husbands and lovers, many of which had died suddenly
and mysteriously. She referred to the photos as "The
Gallery of My Romantic Homicides."

Whether or not Libby Holman had anything to do
with the deaths is uncertain. Her friend, Tallulah Bankhead, said, "I don't think she actually killed all of those
people. But they were kind of set up, as though their
deaths were meant to be."

Libby's most famous romance occurred when she
was in her fifties. Montgomery Clift, sixteen years her
junior, was one of the most handsome and talented
actors in Hollywood. Clift was fascinated by Libby
Holman's lurid past. He was a homosexual and Libby

was one of the few women who attracted him. Libby warned him about being involved with her, "Watch out! Something terrible is going to happen."

Holman referred to herself as Clift's "protectress" but he openly admitted that he was having an affair with the older woman. Clift carried an X-ray of Libby's skull which he kept in a shadow box. He displayed it proudly to his friends, exclaiming, "That's my steady."

It was thought Libby Holman had Montgomery Clift under a spell. She wanted to possess him. They sometimes kissed so violently that their lips bled. They had an almost mystical attraction and seemed to communicate telepathically. A friend, Augusta McCarthy, wrote: "They seemed to be speaking in a language I could not understand." Sometimes Clift crawled on his hands and knees and told Libby how gorgeous she was.

Libby Holman maintained a special room at Treetops which was a personal shrine to Montgomery Clift. It was always kept in readiness for his frequent visits. When Montgomery Clift met Libby he only drank milk, but at Treetops he found marijuana, cocaine, and mescaline in abundance. They visited Havana and attended porn shows, strip joints, and brothels. Montgomery Clift, his beautiful face disfigured in an automobile accident, slowly self-destructed and died in 1966 at age forty-five. Like so many others close to Libby Holman, death came early.

Eventually, she lost her closest friend, Clifton Webb. He was always complaining about his ever-present mother, Mabelle. Libby, tired of hearing his constant complaints, suggested, "Why don't you chloroform the old cunt." Webb never spoke to her again and said, as far as he was concerned, Libby Holman died that night.

Thereafter, he referred to her as the "Black Angel of Death."

In her later years, Libby Holman tried to assume a more normal lifestyle. She became involved in the civil rights movement and was a strong supporter of Dr. Martin Luther King. King was a guest at Treetops and she provided him with the money to visit India where he studied the nonviolent preachings of Mahatma Gandhi.

On June 21, 1971, the bikini clad body of sixty-seven-year-old Libby Holman was found slumped in the front seat of her Rolls-Royce. Like so many others in her life, she died mysteriously. She left a fortune estimated at $12 million. The black angel of death had finally visited Libby Holman.

18

Mexican Spitfire

After her Broadway debacle, Lupe Velez returned to Hollywood to renew her film career. RKO offered her the starring role in *The Girl From Mexico,* a B movie which was tailor-made for her. In it she played Carmelita, a short-tempered south-of-the-border firecracker, not unlike her real life personality. *The Girl From Mexico* was the first of eight "Mexican Spitfire" movies she would star in between 1939 and 1943. The "Mexican Spitfire" series marked both the highlight and lowlight of her career. They reestablished her as a box office attraction and are the films for which she is best remembered. However, for Lupe, they were a reminder that she had been relegated to B movies— programmers, as the studios referred to them.

The slapstick plot of the film had Dennis (Donald Woods), a Manhattan advertising executive, searching for a Latin to sing on his client's radio program. He discovers Carmelita (Lupe Velez) who fractures the English language with Spanish colloquialisms and

causes mayhem wherever she goes. Dennis falls in love
with Carmelita, much to the chagrin of his upper-crust
fiancée, Elizabeth (Linda Hayes). Only Uncle Matt
(veteran rubbered-legged comedian Leon Errol) sides
with Carmelita who overcomes all obstacles and marries Dennis.

The Girl From Mexico, which premiered in New
York on June 7 1939, was a pleasant surprise to RKO.
The Times review noted: "Lupe sings and dances, too,
which does nothing to lower the temperature." Critic
Bosley Crowther also observed that "Loopy Lupe does
it gaily, temptingly, with the natural endowments possessed by her.

Lupe was signed by RKO to a $1,500 a week con-
tract, a third of her peak salary. She had to supplement
her income with personal appearance tours for which
she earned up to $4,000 per week. From the success of
The Girl From Mexico, she was rushed into a sequel,
Mexican Spitfire.

This time, Dennis tries to land a big advertising
contract with stuffy British whiskey magnate, Lord
Epping (Leon Errol in a dual role). Dennis ex-fiancée,
Elizabeth, schemes to embarrass Carmelita, hoping
that he will return to her. She is aided by Dennis'
snooty Aunt Della (Elisabeth Risdon) who disapproves
of Carmelita. Uncle Matt poses as Lord Epping to try
to help along the deal which results in repeated cases
of mistaken identity.

When Carmelita and Uncle Matt accidentally jeop-
ardize the deal, they flee to Mexico where Carmelita
obtains a divorce from Dennis, unaware that it is not
valid. Dennis hears the news and becomes engaged
again to Elizabeth. Now realizing she and Dennis are

still married, Carmelita returns to New York just in
time to stop the wedding. The movie ends with Carmelita and Elizabeth engaged in a free-for-all food
fight.

The New York Times film critic, Frank Nugent, approved of the slapstick confection, comparing it with
Mack Sennett's Keystone comedies. Leon Errol, in his
double role as Uncle Matt and Lord Epping, particularly stole the show. The veteran Australian comic
had perfected his craft in medicine shows, vaudeville,
and the *Ziegfeld Follies*, before coming to Hollywood.
His portrayal of the stiff-necked, rubber-legged Lord
Epping was inspired comedy.

During the filming of *Mexican Spitfire*, Lupe's voracious appetite nearly did her in. Despite weighing only
112 pounds, Lupe ate almost everything in sight.
Whenever one of her films had a scene with food on
the set, a guard was posted to keep Lupe away. In the
climactic scene of *Mexican Spitfire*, thirty cream pies
were placed on the table to be used in the food fight.
Before shooting began, the assistant director discovered Lupe in the midst of gulping down her fourth pie.

"What have you done, Lupe?" he asked.

"I have just eaten a little, four of them, I think, why?"

"Heavens above! They've been sprayed with fly spray
to keep the bugs off them. They're not for eating.
You'll die."

Lupe survived, and RKO, hoping to capitalize on her
newly found popularity, planned to reteam her with
Victor McLaglen, her costar in *Hot Pepper*, in *The
Marines Fly High*, but the project fell through. Instead,
she was cast in *Mexican Spitfire Out West*. The now-
familiar plot had Dennis trying to secure a million-

dollar advertising account from Lord Epping. Carmelita believes she is being neglected and goes to Reno to get a divorce. After a series of comic misunderstandings, Carmelita and Dennis are reconciled and his advertising firm is awarded the lucrative contract.

The New York Times was less than complimentary this time in its appraisal: "Lupe Velez, whose explosive performances are beginning to sound like Donald Duck. . . . Although she has less to do, Miss Velez makes up for it by playing at the top of her lungs."

Much of the humor in the "Mexican Spitfire" series was improvisational. Lupe Velez explained, "I wrote much of those last comedies. I ad-libbed most of all of our lines. Like this—we come on the set and someone says, 'Oke doke, Lupe, you are mad at your husband in this scene, see?' So you say what I think will be funny and, there you are! You look at the shooting script yourself, most every line is a question mark—we do the dialogue!"

In June 1940 *Silver Screen* featured an article about Lupe Velez entitled "She Heet De Bool's Eye!" Writer William Vallee proclaimed: "Lupe Velez, again a terrific box-office sensation, doesn't mind discussing her life, be it public or private, and does so with her priceless sense of humor."

Between films, Lupe headlined a show at New York's Paramount Theater with Red Skelton and Tommy Dorsey and his Orchestra. The hour-long stage show went on between showings of the feature, and Lupe performed three times a day during the scheduled two-week engagement.

Backstage, Lupe liked to sniff scallions. She told an interviewer what happened when she gave some of the scallions to Skelton. "I handed them to Red Skelton today in the show instead of the flowers, and what did he did, the dog? He ate one and blew it in my face! I think he is a second Bob Hope, that one! Our show is supposed to run sixty minutes but every day it runs ninety or so."

Between shows, a chain-smoking Lupe could be found playing solitaire on the bed. From backstage she would count the crowd. Lupe joked, "We don't let any of our customers leave — if they start, we jump down from the stage after them — seven feet that drop is." Her sense of humor took a bizarre turn. "Then, I think, I get a shotgun and when I come on stage I say, 'What do you know, people? There has been a murder in the balcony. No one knew it! Ha! Ha!'"

During the movies, Lupe Velez and Red Skelton came out on stage and heckled the actors on screen. The audiences loved it and they were held over a record six weeks.

Lupe was determined to get Red Skelton into bed. As author Arthur Marx noted, she usually got her man: "In show business circles, Lupe Velez's reputation for being a nymphomaniac was one of the worst-kept secrets of the century. There was hardly a leading man with whom the Mexican Spitfire had ever worked that she didn't eventually succeed in luring into bed."

Red Skelton wore long underwear backstage between shows. The underwear had an open window flap in the back and Lupe chased Red with a stick, trying to unflap his long johns. Eventually, Lupe had her way and Skelton admitted to a friend that he slept with her between shows.

Lupe, who was thirty-two years old at the time, al-

ways insisted she was four years younger. She rea-
soned, in a logic only Lupe understood, that her
mother would have to be 120 years old if she was thirty-
two. She explained that her carefree lifestyle kept her
young. "Why worry? You worry and it gets you nowhere. We all get old anyway and if you fret you just
get older all the quicker. That's why I look so young as I
am—I relax. And I am not that old!"

She did a scathing impersonation of Adolf Hitler but
rarely performed it in public because she believed poli-
tics and show business didn't mix. Her friends urged
Lupe to write a book of her colloquialisms which she
called "silly sayings" but the project never materialized.

In South America and Mexico, Lupe Velez's popularity was second only to Greta Garbo's. To take advan-
tage of Velez-mania, *Recordar Es Visir*, a compilation of
Mexican films featuring Arturo de Cordova, Cantinflas, and Lupe Velez (in scenes from *La Zandunga*),
was released in her homeland.

For a time, Lupe Velez set up residence in Mexico
City. While there, she came under investigation by the
FBI, thanks to her old enemy, the Countess di Frasso.
Because of her connections with Mussolini, the
Countess was under constant surveillance as a possible
spy. In 1941, she leased a hacienda in the capital,
which was considered a haven for international spy
rings.

A FBI report from September 1941, demonstrated
their concern with the Countess: "Subject reportedly
now living in Mexico City . . . building a pretentious
villa at Acapulco, Mexico. . . . Subject has been out of
the limelight in Hollywood society since May. She is
notorious for her nymphomaniac propensities, lech-

erous parties, and publicity seeking, also for being close
to Mussolini . . . reportedly friendly with Cary Grant
and [Barbara] Hutton recently in Mexico City and pre-
sumed to have been subject's guests. Theory advanced
by one informant that di Frasso may be financed by
Mexican government to draw Hollywood film stars to
Mexico City. . . ."

The connection between the Countess di Frasso and
Lupe Velez was Barbara Hutton. Woolworth heiress
Hutton was the second richest woman in the world,
behind tobacco heiress, Doris Duke. Dubbed the "Poor
Little Rich Girl" by the press, she made headlines due
to her unhappy personal life. Her inheritance, the
equivalent of a billion dollar fortune today, made her
the target of playboys, gigolos, and penniless counts
and pauper princes. These not-so-noblemen usually
insisted on million dollar dowries and multimillion dollar divorce settlements. "I won't say my husbands
thought only of my money, but it had a certain fascina-
tion for them," she acknowledged.

Criticized for renouncing her American citizenship,
Hutton claimed she did it for tax purposes but the
public never forgave her. During the Depression, she
was attacked by a man who screamed, "You rich bitch!
I'd like to throw acid in your face."

Her latest romance was with Cary Grant. The press
labeled the pair "Cash and Cary" and hounded them
wherever they went. The FBI put them under surveillance after they stayed with the Countess di Frasso.
Their hotel room was bugged and anyone they visited
was under suspicion. Unfortunately, Hutton and Grant
visited Lupe Velez and she too came under FBI investigation. The agency was especially suspicious of her

because of their belief that the Mexican government was trying to lure movie stars to Mexico City and because she had been previously investigated as a Communist.

The FBI continued looking into the Countess di Frasso but never uncovered any evidence against her, Lupe Velez, or Barbara Hutton and Cary Grant, who wed in 1942. The marriage didn't last but Grant had the distinction of being the only one of Hutton's seven husbands not to ask for alimony. Barbara Hutton summed up her life when she said, "Money alone can't bring you happiness."

Back in Hollywood, Lupe Velez and Leon Errol were loaned to Universal for *Six Lessons From Madame La Zonga* (1941). The title was derived from a popular song. The thin plot had Lupe Velez in the title role as a loud-mouth Cuban nightclub performer who is hired to transform New Yorker Helen Parrish into a Latin singing sensation.

The shipboard comedy featured William Frawley (the longtime actor who later gained fame as Fred Mertz on *I Love Lucy*) and former Stooge, Shemp Howard. Playing a supporting role as a cowboy named Alvin was Guinn "Big Boy" Williams, veteran of dozens of movies, usually playing the not-so-bright sidekick in Westerns. "Big Boy" got his nickname because of his hulking 250-pound frame. Bow-legged and rubber-faced, with small eyes and light hair, Williams had the reputation of being one of the best polo players in Hollywood. His Uplifters Club Polo Team won numerous trophies.

Lupe Velez was always attracted to muscular men and she fell hard for "Big Boy." In November 1940, she had announced her engagement to him. His best friends were Errol Flynn and Alan Hale, Sr. Flynn was known as the "Colonel," Hale was the "Sergeant," and Williams was the "Corporal." These three hellraisers were the holy terrors of the Hollywood night life.

For some unknown reasons, "Big Boy" Williams hated Orson Welles, who had recently arrived in Hollywood sporting a newly grown beard. "Big Boy" hated the beard even more than he hated Welles. To show his displeasure, he sent Welles a ham with a beard on it.

One evening, "Big Boy" Williams, Errol Flynn, John Barrymore, and Pat O'Brien were having dinner at Mike Romanoff's when Welles made a dramatic entrance. Welles had always wanted to meet Barrymore so Pat O'Brien, unaware of "Big Boy's" dislike, invited him to their table. Barrymore was so drunk that when he heard the name Orson Welles he thought it was the name of a new watering hole in town.

During the introduction "Big Boy" began to tighten up, his object of scorn was within arm's distance. Suddenly, he blurted out, "You stupid looking bastard."

Welles tried to ignore the insult but "Big Boy" persisted, "In all my goddamn life I have never seen a more hammy, stupid-looking piece of blubber than you."

Not satisfied, "Big Boy" decided to test if the beard was real by pulling on it. Welles' patience ran out and he said, "Sir, obviously we had better go outside and settle this." Impressed by Welles' courage, Errol Flynn stepped in before the two men came to blows, probably saving Hollywood's "Boy Wonder" from a beating.

Errol Flynn was fascinated with Lupe Velez's sexuality. Flynn was Hollywood's most notorious lover and the cry, "In like Flynn," became synonymous with sexual promiscuity. It was estimated that Flynn had four thousand sexual encounters in his life and that figure may be conservative. Flynn liked to put a pinch of cocaine on the tip of his penis as an aphrodisiac and had one-way mirrors installed in his home so he could watch his guests make love.

Lupe Velez did one trick with her body that Flynn had never seen anyone else do. She was able to rotate her left breast and then counter-rotate it. Flynn was impressed by her dexterity and remarked, "It was so supple and beautiful you couldn't believe your eyes."

Despite his size and reputation as a mauler, "Big Boy" Williams did have a sensitive side. If his feelings were hurt he would cry like a baby. Errol Flynn commented that Lupe Velez and "Big Boy" Williams were the oddest couple he had ever seen. They were always arguing and, although Lupe was a foot-and-a-half shorter and 150 pounds lighter than Williams, she was more than a match for him in a fight.

One of their most violent quarrels took place at Errol Flynn's home. Lupe, in a rage, picked up a large, framed photograph of "Big Boy" and beat him over the head with it until she broke the frame and nearly broke his head. She removed the photo, tore it into little pieces, and threw the pieces on the floor. As a final gesture, she urinated on "Big Boy's" photograph. This represented the end of their beautiful relationship. Lupe began seeing other men, including Clayton Moore of "Lone Ranger" fame.

Though working steadily, Lupe Velez continued to pressure RKO for better roles. She argued that her popularity was at an all-time high. The studio, which was making sizable profits on the low-budget "Mexican Spitfire" films, was reluctant to scuttle the series but promised better parts for Lupe if she agreed to one more film.

That would be *Mexican Spitfire's Baby* (1941). Leon Errol returned as Uncle Matt but Charles "Buddy" Rogers replaced Donald Woods as Carmelita's long-suffering husband, Dennis. The story has Carmelita and Dennis adopting a European war orphan which turns out to be a blonde bombshell played by curvaceous Marion Martin. Fluttery ZaSu Pitts was brought into this "Mexican Spitfire" entry to provide added byplay with Leon Errol.

The principal distinction of *Mexican Spitfire's Baby* was that it played on the same bill with the film many people consider the greatest of all time, *Citizen Kane*.

William Randolph Hearst had pressured the Rockefellers not to allow *Citizen Kane* to premier at Radio City Music Hall, which to that time was the showcase for RKO's top films. The movie was shunted to the RKO Palace on Broadway, which showed the studio's lesser fare, and it opened there on May 1, 1941. Despite rave reviews, the film did poorly at the box-office because Hearst's newspapers refused to accept advertising. *Mexican Spitfire's Baby*, on the lower half of the bill, suffered the same fate as its more illustrious counterpart.

Lupe Velez had another reason to resent Orson Welles. Because the European market had been eliminated by World War II, the South American and Mexican markets became especially lucrative. Latin actresses like Lupe Velez, Dolores Del Rio, and Carmen

Miranda were in great demand. At the time, Orson
Welles was having a torrid affair with Dolores Del Rio.
He was particularly fascinated with Del Rio's hand-
made panties which he claimed were practically nonex-
istent. Because of Welles' prestige, his lover, Dolores
Del Rio, naturally was given the preferred Latin roles
at RKO at the expense of Lupe Velez.

19

The Great Lover

In March 1941, Lupe Velez signed a three film contract extension with RKO. *Playmates* gave her the opportunity to play opposite the legendary but now in his cups John Barrymore. He had once been considered the greatest actor on the American stage, but his years of drinking and womanizing had left him a caricature of himself.

John Barrymore was born into the most illustrious family of the American theater, known as the "Royal Family of Broadway." His father, Maurice, was a respected stage actor and his brother, Lionel, and sister, Ethel, had distinguished acting careers on the stage and screen.

Incredibly handsome in his youth, John Barrymore earned the nicknames, "The Great Lover" and "The Great Profile." He was seduced by his stepmother when he was fifteen and had a scandalous affair with showgirl Evelyn Nesbit. He seduced seventeen-year-old Mary Astor during the filming of *Beau Brummel* while her mother waited in the adjoining room. His sexual appetite was prodigious. Barrymore once spent a month in a Calcutta brothel. His reputation as a lover was so great that Charlie Chaplin pointed his telescope at Barrymore's bedroom window to observe his sexual exploits.

Originally, John Barrymore made his living as a cartoonist, but once he turned to acting he became a sensation. On stage, he became America's leading Shakespearean actor, and his transition into films was equally impressive. In the silent film, *Dr. Jekyll and Mr. Hyde*, Barrymore made the transformation from Jekyll to Hyde without the use of make up.

He lived life to the fullest. His ninety-three-foot schooner, "The Mariner," set a transpacific speed record. Barrymore's forty-five-room home, Bella Vista, overlooked Sunset Boulevard and featured a stocked trout pond, skeet shooting range, kidney shaped pool, and an aviary with over three hundred exotic birds. Barrymore's favorite part of the house was a frontier bar which he had shipped from Alaska and reassembled.

Barrymore's dogs were kerry blue terriers which he named Shake, Quake, and Shock because they were born during an earthquake. His favorite pet was a vulture named Mahoney. On command, Mahoney would preen his master's moustache and eyebrows. Barrymore rewarded the bird with a kiss on the beak.

At the height of his fame, John Barrymore married the beautiful actress, Dolores Costello. Barrymore said of her, "She was the most preposterously lovely creature in the world, a charming child, slender and shy and golden haired." He was shattered when Costello's beautiful face was partially disfigured by improperly applied makeup.

His drinking became out of control. He was so desperate for alcohol that he drank his wife's perfume. His family and friends tried to keep alcohol away from him to no avail. When all liquor was removed from his yacht, the pathetic Barrymore drank alcohol he siphoned off from the ship's cooling system. He became paranoid and believed his cook was trying to poison his soup.

His reputation as a great lover also suffered. He made animal sounds in a pitiful attempt to seduce Tallulah Bankhead. He co-starred with Katharine Hepburn in her first film, A Bill of Divorcement. Barrymore invited the young actress into his dressing room where she found him completely naked. When she resisted his advances, Barrymore said, "My dear, any young girl would be thrilled to make love to the great John Barrymore."

"Not me," Hepburn replied, and left the room.

On his 55th birthday, a few of his friends sent him a nude girl wrapped in cellophane. He was terrified of being buried alive because he frequently collapsed after his bouts with alcohol. He urinated in public and during his stage performance he forgot his lines and sometimes vomited. Some people came to the theater just to watch him fall down. His once great performances became self parody. "I am doing the work of a whore," he said. "There is nothing as sad in the world as an old prostitute."

The extent of his personal and financial problems became apparent to everyone in September 1938, when he was forced to sell his beloved estate, Bella

Vista. Although the estate had cost millions, it sold for only $90,000. Hollywood was shocked. If it could happen to John Barrymore, it could happen to anyone.

The story line of *Playmates* was the ultimate humiliation. Barrymore played himself, an ex-matinee idol who owes back taxes to the IRS. He admits, "I've been in the public eye so long it's permanently bloodshot." Barrymore is offered a lucrative radio contract by a vitamin sponsor on the condition that he teach bandleader Kay Kyser to play Shakespeare. After hearing Kyser recite the Bard's work in his thick North Carolina accent, he realizes that the task is impossible.

Lupe Velez plays Carmen del Torre, the world's greatest woman bullfighter. Angry with Barrymore because he jilted her, she bursts into his room and throws a hairpin which just misses his head. She chokes him, pulls his hair, and twists his nose, exclaiming, "I'm going to kill you until you're dead!" Once he calms her down, he asks her to cause Kay Kyser to have a nervous breakdown. "A man has never lived who I can't make suffer," she boasts.

Lupe tries unsuccessfully to seduce Kay Kyser. To make Kyser lose his voice, Barrymore puts a solution in his drink but by mistake, gulps down the doctored beverage himself and is laughed off the stage when he is unable to speak. Kay Kyser and his Orchestra perform "Shakespeare in Swing" while Lupe chases the mute Barrymore.

The deteriorating status of John Barrymore's reputation was evidenced by the fact that Kay Kyser received top billing. Even the ads for *Playmates* mocked Barrymore's reputation as a Lothario, with Lupe Velez looking at Barrymore and asking, "Me play second fiddle to that model-T Romeo?" The ad's announced that the cast was headed by this Mexican Mickey Finn (Lupe Velez) and promised viewers would see "Kay go goofy over Lupe."

Lupe made the most of her role, especially her scintillating Conga number. The *Baltimore Evening Sun* wrote: "She makes Carmen Miranda, who also makes such dances a specialty, by comparison seem as retiring as little Elsie Dinsmore of the nursery books."

The movie opened in New York on Christmas Day 1941 and *The Times* reviewer was appalled by the treatment of John Barrymore. "It may be amusing to some people to witness the spectacle of John Barrymore making a buffoon of himself on the screen but this spectator for one fails to see the humor of it."

Playmates would be John Barrymore's last film. During filming he broke down and wept when he was forced to recite "To be or not to be," to Ish Kabibble, the fright-wigged buffoon in Kay Kyser's band. Shortly after completing *Playmates*, guest star Barrymore was providing comedy relief on Rudy Vallee's radio program on May 19, 1941, when he collapsed during the broadcast. Suffering from congestion of the lungs and cirrhosis of the liver, he lapsed in and out of a coma. Nearing the end, Barrymore came out of the coma and saw an especially homely nurse.

"Well get into bed, anyway," he told her. John Barrymore died on May 29. It was said that he was the victim of the longest suicide on record. He had sixty cents in his pocket when he collapsed.

According to the story told by Errol Flynn and director, Raoul Walsh, Barrymore gave his final performance after death. Flynn and Walsh were having a wake for Barrymore at the Cock and Bull Bar on Sunset Boulevard when Walsh came up with an idea for a practical joke. He excused himself, and with the help of two accomplices, went to the mortuary, where they bribed the attendant to borrow Barrymore's body for the evening. They placed the body in Errol Flynn's favorite chair facing the front door. When Flynn opened the door of his home the first thing he saw was the puffy, white face of John Barrymore staring at him. Flynn, a fearless man who had once been a diamond smuggler and stood trial for murder in New Guinea, let out a blood curdling scream and ran from the room.

Most of the spectators who went to Barrymore's funeral were there to see the famous stars in attendance such as Clark Gable, Spencer Tracy, and Errol Flynn. His remaining possessions went on the auction block. Edgar Bergen paid $185 for his collection of Ecuadorian shrunken heads. A John Singer Sargent painting went for the rock bottom price of $250. John Barrymore's girdle sold for $4.50.

Lupe Velez next was loaned to Columbia for *Honolulu Lu*, opposite Leo Carrillo, standing in for Leon Errol, it seems. Also in the cast were up-and-coming Columbia contract players Forrest Tucker and Lloyd Bridges, and silent film comedian, Chester Conklin. Lupe played Consuelo Cordoba, the niece of Don Esteban (Leo Carrillo). She wins the local personality contest and becomes Honolulu Lu, the scatterbrained sweetheart of the fleet. Lupe sang Sammy Cahn-Saul Chaplin songs and mimicked Katharine Hepburn and Gloria Swanson. The timing of the release of *Honolulu Lu* (December 11, 1941) couldn't have been worse, just four days after the attack on Pearl Harbor. Understandably, America was not in the mood for a comedy set in

Honolulu, even if it did have the clowning of Lupe Velez.

Back at RKO, Lupe was rushed into three more "Mexican Spitfire" movies in 1942. The first, *Mexican Spitfire at Sea*, has Dennis taking Carmelita on a second honeymoon cruise. She has a fit when she learns that the real reason for the cruise is to try as usual to land a big advertising contract.

Mexican Spitfire Sees a Ghost, which was released a mere four weeks later, was more of the same. It concerned a hectic night at a haunted country estate. Leon Errol was called on to play three characters: Uncle Matt, Lord Epping, and Epping's valet, Hubbell. He ended up getting most of the critical attention with *The New York Times* saying of Lupe Velez merely that "as Mr. Errol's ebullient niece, [she] lends her gnarled phraseology to the proceedings."

Mexican Spitfire's Elephant was only slightly better than its predecessors. Lord Epping (Leon Errol) is tricked into smuggling a small elephant figurine which contains a precious gem. He forgets where he leaves the elephant and the plot concerns the jewel thieves' efforts to find it. The highlight occurs when Carmelita (Lupe Velez) mistakenly believes they are searching for a real elephant. She tries to help by bringing a real elephant (with pink and green spots) into a cafe, a sight which causes the drunks to give up alcohol.

Mexican Spitfire's Elephant, while it will never be compared to *The Maltese Falcon*, did receive decent reviews. *Variety* wrote: "The latest in the Lupe Velez-Leon Errol Mexican Spitfire series is a solid laugh entertainment and the best of the group."

Lupe Velez's latest boyfriend was quite a contrast to "Big Boy" Williams and certainly a change of pace.

Intellectual Erich Maria Remarque was one of the most respected novelists of his time. His international bestseller, *All Quiet on the Western Front,* was one of the first antiwar novels and was made into an Academy Award winning film.

Remarque was wounded five times during World War I and suffered permanent lung damage. After the war, he drifted through a variety of odd jobs including being a salesman for a tombstone company, organist in an insane asylum, and a test driver. He began his writing career as the editor of *Sportbild,* an illustrated sports magazine in Germany which predated *Sports Illustrated* by thirty years.

The publication of *All Quiet on the Western Front* made Remarque a world celebrity but its antiwar message made him a marked man in Nazi Germany. In 1938, he was stripped of his German citizenship and his books were burned. The following year he moved to the United States and later became a citizen.

Although Remarque was a distinguished writer, he looked more like a halfback on a football team. Tall, blond, and handsome, he possessed an athletic appearance that made him popular with women. He was an avid modern art collector and owned several Van Goghs and Cezannes.

Lupe Velez tried to change her image to please Remarque. She dyed her hair blonde and tried to conduct herself in a more sophisticated manner. Erich Remarque was Lupe's regular escort on the nightclub circuit in Hollywood and New York. Eventually, the couple drifted apart and Remarque later married actress Paulette Goddard.

20

Suicide at the Casa Felicitas

Astrologers were very popular in Hollywood in the 1940s, one of the most famous psychics being Blanca Holmes. It was trendy for stars to have their fortunes read and Lupe Velez visited Holmes, who during the reading, was visibly upset and refused to tell Lupe what she saw in her future. After Lupe's insistence, Holmes reluctantly revealed that she had been born under the tragic fixed star, Proscyn. "The stars say you will commit suicide with poison," she told a shaken Lupe.

The dire prediction had a noticeable effect on Lupe Velez. She had always lived in a carefree manner and never thought about death. Her friends told her to disregard the deathly prediction, but she took it seriously and never forgot it.

Ladies Day was not officially a "Mexican Spitfire" movie but the film shared many of the same elements. It was directed by Leslie Goodwins, who had done all the "Mexican Spitfire" films. Lupe (in a blonde wig) played Pepita, a former burlesque queen who marries major league pitcher, Wacky Walker, played by Eddie Albert. Walker is so love-smitten that he can't pitch when Pepita is around. Believing Pepita to be too much of a distraction, Walker's teammates and their wives, led by Patsy Kelly, kidnap her before he takes the mound for the big game, but have a devil of a time keeping the spitfire bound and gagged.

Lupe's co-star, Eddie Albert, was born Eddie Heimberger but changed his name because everybody called him "Hamburger." He originally wanted to be an insurance agent but turned to acting after selling only one policy (to his father). His acting career has spanned a half century and, although he earned two Oscar nominations (*Roman Holiday, The Heartbreak Kid*) for his work in film, he is best remembered for his role as Oliver Douglas on the television situation comedy, Green Acres.

Ex-heavyweight champion, Max Baer, had a major role in the film as Fatso, one of the ballplayers. The son of a butcher, Baer became a boxer at age nineteen after knocking out a cowboy with one punch during a brawl. Blessed with a tremendous physique and incredible punching power, he quickly became a contender for the heavyweight title. In 1930, boxer Frankie Campbell died after a match with Baer and, two years later, Ernie Schaaf suffered a brain hemorrhage in a fight with him and died after his next bout.

Baer began to clown his way through fights, fearful that his deadly right hand might kill another opponent. Sportswriters called him "The Magnificent Screwball" and "Madcap Maxie." One boxing scribe described him as "the man with the million dollar body and ten cent brain."

Despite his image as a killer, Baer was terrified of mice. During the filming of *The Prizefighter and the Lady*, director Woody Van Dyke left a mouse on his chair. When Baer saw the mouse he let out a scream and ran off the set.

On June 14, 1934, Max Baer fought champion Primo Carnera for the heavyweight title. Carnera, at six-foot-six and 260 pounds, was the biggest heavyweight champion in boxing history. Baer proved the old boxing adage, "the bigger they are, the harder they fall," when he knocked Carnera down a record twelve times before stopping him in the eleventh round. Once, Carnera pulled Baer down with him on his way to the canvas. Baer sprang to his feet and yelled, "Last one up is a sissy."

A year later, Baer lost his title to the "Cinderella Man," James Braddock in one of boxing's biggest upsets. On his weekly radio program, Baer commented, "Jim can use the title. He has five kids. I don't know how many I have." The remark cost him his radio show but he still commanded up to $8,000 a week in vaudeville. He made the transition to movies without a hitch and appeared in several films before his death in 1959. Baer was especially effective as a bloodthirsty boxer in Humphrey Bogart's last film, *The Harder They Fall*. His son, Max Baer, Jr., played Jethro Bodine on *The Beverly Hillbillies*.

By 1943, Lupe Velez's acting had become self parody and she often substituted volume for technique. *The New York Times* was not too kind in its appraisal of her performance in *Ladies Day*: "Miss Velez doesn't act too well, but she acts loud; her display of Latin temperament resembles the law of molecular motion."

Mexican Spitfire's Blessed Event was the eighth and final entry of the "Mexican Spitfire" series. Walter Reed replaced Buddy Rogers in the role of Carmelita's husband, Dennis Lindsay. Also in the cast as Dennis' rival, Mr. Sharpe, was Hugh Beaumont (Ward Cleaver years later on the long-running television series, *Leave It to Beaver*).

In this poor man's version of *Bringing Up Baby*, Uncle Matt gives Carmelia a pet ocelot. As usual, Dennis is trying to land a big advertising contract with millionaire Lord Epping, who is hunting moose at a remote lodge. As he is about to sign Dennis' contract, Mr. Sharpe shows up unexpectedly.

At this moment, Dennis receives a message from Carmelita that she has had a "blessed event," which he naturally assumes to be a baby and not a baby ocelot. Lord Epping promises to sign Dennis' contract after he sees the baby.

They travel to Arizona, where Carmelita is staying. When they ask Lupe about the baby, there is some amusing dialogue.

"Is it a boy or a girl?"

"I don't know what it is but I'll find out for you."

"What color eyes does the baby have?"

"Yellow. But it's got brown spots all over it."

Lord Epping gives Carmelita twenty-four hours to produce the baby or he'll make a deal with Mr. Sharpe. Carmelita poses as a nurse to "borrow" someone else's baby. She is able to fool Lord Epping and, at the end of the movie, discovers she is really pregnant.

Lupe's next film, *Redhead From Manhattan*, would be her last American movie. Columbia's advertising campaign guaranteed that the film would "knock you for a Lupe," but failed to deliver on its promise. Lupe appeared in the dual role as Rita, a zany ship stowaway, and her pregnant cousin, musical star, Elaine Manners.

After making *Redhead From Manhattan*, Lupe Velez broke off contract talks with RKO. Ironically, the struggling studio wanted to focus its limited resources on making Tarzan movies featuring its newly signed star, Johnny Weissmuller. Lupe Velez was humiliated and announced she was leaving Hollywood forever to make films in Mexico.

In October 1943, she began a version of Emile Zola's *Nana* at the Aztec Studio in Mexico City. She played the title role of the Parisian streetwalker. (The film premiered in Mexico City in June 1944 to very good reviews—the best of Lupe's career.) When Lupe returned to Hollywood shortly before Christmas 1943, she told everyone that her performance would reestablish her as a serious dramatic actress.

Since her divorce from Weissmuller, Lupe had gone through, as Kenneth Anger noted in *Hollywood Babylon II*, a "small army of lovers." As she got older and her star diminished, her lovers were gigolos or stuntmen instead of the leading men with whom she had been involved with in her prime. Her latest (and last) lover was Harald Ramond.

Ramond was a darkly handsome twenty-seven-year old French actor. He had served for two years as a partisan fighter but was captured and imprisoned in the concentration camp at Dachau, where he made a daring escape.

He was an unemployed bit actor in Hollywood when he met Lupe Velez in 1943. Lupe claimed that her romance with Gary Cooper had been "kid stuff" compared with her new love. "Harald certainly knows how to handle me. I've always been used to controlling men, but I try it with Harald and he tells me where to go." It appeared that she had finally met a man who could tame her.

Lupe insisted that she had no immediate plans for marriage. Her bad memories of her marriage with Johnny Weissmuller were still fresh. She told reporter Mary Morris, "I don't believe in marriage, darling. If there's children, okay. But to a woman who has a career it means here today and gone tomorrow. . . . I'm just being practical when I say husband and career don't mix."

Lupe's next project was a Broadway musical, *Glad to See You,* with former child star Jane Withers and Eddie Foy, Jr. It would give Lupe the opportunity to work with the legendary choreographer and director, Busby Berkeley.

Berkeley overcame personal problems to become the top choreographer in show business. Prior to coming to Hollywood, Berkeley had worked in a shoe factory in Massachusetts. During World War I, he served as a lieutenant in the artillery. Berkeley worked out a trick drill for 1,200 men and discovered his love of choreography.

In the 1930s Busby Berkeley choreographed some of Warner Bros.' most dazzling musicals, including *42nd Street* and the *Golddigger* movies. His incredible synchronized dance routines with their kaleidoscopic effects set the standard for Hollywood production numbers. Berkeley was instrumental in promoting the careers of many young stars including Lucille Ball, Veronica Lake, and Paulette Goddard.

His career appeared to be over in 1935 when he was involved in a near-fatal automobile accident. Berkeley was driving home from a party on the twisting Pacific Coast Highway when his left front tire blew out. He lost control of his car and slammed head-on into another vehicle, killing its three occupants. The unconscious Berkeley was dragged from his burning automobile. While still hospitalized, he was charged with three counts of manslaughter. During the sensational trial, Berkeley was wheeled into the courtroom on a stretcher. Two trials ended in hung juries before he was finally acquitted.

Busby Berkeley regained his preeminence and directed a number of successful Broadway and Hollywood musicals. Lupe Velez looked forward to working with Busby Berkeley and the songwriting team of Sammy Cahn and Jule Styne.

Rehearsals for *Glad to See You* were scheduled to begin in October 1944, but the show was doomed from the start. When Lupe Velez arrived in New York she was outraged that no one connected with the production was there to meet her at the station. She was accustomed to being greeted by reporters and being sent flowers by the producer. Furiously, she phoned Busby Berkeley and informed him she was returning to Hollywood, and that if he was smart he would join her.

After Lupe's departure, the show collapsed, folding in Boston before it reached Broadway. For Berkeley, it was the beginning of renewed personal problems which resulted in a complete mental breakdown. Busby Berkeley slashed his wrists and was confined to a psychiatric ward for six weeks. It would be years before he was able to return to Hollywood and his career never fully recovered.

Lupe Velez was facing her own personal problems. On November 27, 1944, she announced that she was engaged to be married to Harald Ramond. "I think I marry him," she told reporters. The reason for her change of heart was that she learned that she was three months pregnant. She announced the engagement without the knowledge of her fiancé. She figured that once he learned that she was pregnant that he would be honored to marry her.

When Lupe told Ramond that she was pregnant, she was stunned when he refused to marry her. Her tremendous pride was deeply hurt and she realized that the scandal of being an unwed mother in Hollywood could ruin her career. She was hysterical when she phoned Bo Roos, her manager. Roos was concerned by the desperation in her voice and made her promise not to do anything drastic. He confronted Harald Ramond and asked, "What do you intend to do about it?"

Ramond's solution was to agree to marry Lupe Velez, solely to give her baby a name. He insisted on having a document prepared which Lupe would have to sign. When Lupe heard about his proposal, she was furious. On December 10, she telephoned Louella Parsons and informed her that the engagement was off. Incredibly, she blamed their breakup on a post-election disagreement. No mention was made of the baby. She told Parsons, "I told him to get out. I like my dogs better!" When Louella asked Lupe how to spell Ramond's name she replied, "I don't know. I never did know. Who cares?"

Because she was a devout Catholic, she never considered having an abortion. She briefly contemplated asking one of her sisters to claim the child but abandoned the plan. She told her trusted friend, Adela Rogers St. Johns, "I am confused. Things happen like I do not expect. Say the prayer for me."

On December 11, Lupe went to the Trocadero, the scene of so many joyous evenings. She was uncharacteristically depressed.

"I know I'm not worth anything. I can't sing well. I can't dance," she said.

Two nights later, Lupe attended the Hollywood premier of *Nana* with her best friend, Estelle Taylor, and Benita (Mrs. Jack) Oakie. It should have been one of the highlights of Lupe Velez's career. Many of the reviews called *Nana* Lupe's greatest dramatic performance. Lupe was inconsolable and said to Estelle Taylor, "I am getting to the point where the only thing I am afraid of is life itself. I am just weary with the whole world. People think I like to fight. I have to fight for everything. I'm so tired of it all. Ever since I was a baby I've been fighting. I've never met a man with whom I didn't have to fight to exist."

She returned to her home, the Casa Felicitas ("Happy Home"), with Taylor and Oakie. They celebrated the successful premier with a spectacular Mexican dinner. Lupe was depressed and reminisced about her life and career. "Gary was my big love," she admitted. She confessed to Estelle Taylor that she was pregnant. "I don't know what to do. It's my baby. I couldn't commit murder and still live with myself. I would rather kill myself." When Estelle Taylor and Benita Oakie left around three A.M. they couldn't have realized that they would be the last people to see Lupe Velez alive.

Lupe concluded that the only way out was suicide. She wanted her death to be worthy of a Hollywood star. She looked around at her thirty-foot bedroom. On her dresser were hundreds of bottles of expensive perfumes from all over the world. There was a polar bear skin rug, white satin drapes, carved statues of saints and madonnas, mirrored walls, and the centerpiece of the room, an eight foot bed with a rainbow shaped headboard. The black, silver, and gold lacquers of the headboard contrasted with the otherwise all-white room. Whenever Lupe brought someone into her bedroom she said, "It's the room of a movie star, all right."

Lupe had carefully prepared for her final evening. She had filled the room with beautiful, fragrant gardenias and tuberoses. Dozens of candles were lit. No detail had been overlooked. She had even had her hair and nails done that day.

Lupe put on her favorite blue satin pajamas. She swallowed seventy-five Seconal tablets, washing them down with her finest brandy. Lupe laid her head on the pink satin pillow for the last time. She placed her hands across her breasts, imagining how beautiful she would look the next morning when her body was found.

There are two accounts of what really happened that night. According to the official version, the housekeeper, Juanita, found Lupe on the bed the next morning. A policeman reportedly commented, "She looked so small in that outsized bed that we thought she was a doll." *The Hollywood Reporter* wrote that Lupe Velez was "glamorous to the end."

Louella Parsons devoted her column to Lupe's

death: "Lupe was never lovelier as she lay there, as if slumbering . . . like a child taking nappy. Like a good little girl. Hark! There are the doggies! There's Chops. There's Chips, scratching at the door. They're whispering. They're whining. They want their little Lupe to take them out to play."

A more bizarre story circulated, painting a much different picture of Lupe's death. She had passed out on the bed but the combination of the spicy Mexican meal and the pills made her sick to her stomach. Half conscious, she stumbled toward the bathroom, leaving a trail of vomit on the white carpet. Just as she reached the bathroom, she slipped on the tiles and fell head-first into the toilet. The next day she was discovered lying with her head submerged in her Egyptian Chartreuse Onyx Hush-Flush Model Deluxe commode.

Lupe Velez left two suicide notes in her childlike scrawl. The first was addressed to Harald Ramond, the man who had refused to marry her.

"My God forgive you and forgive me, too, but I prefer to take my life away and our baby's before I bring him shame or kill him. How could you, Harald, fake such a great love for me and our baby when all the time you didn't want us? I see no other way out for me so goodbye and good luck to you.

Love,
Lupe."

The other note was to her friend and housekeeper, Beulah Kinder:

"My faithful friend, you and only you know the fact for the reason I am taking my life. May God forgive me, and don't think bad of me. I love you many. Take care of your mother, so goodbye and try to forgive me.

Say goodbye to all my friends and the American press that were always so nice to me. P.S. Take care of Chips and Chops."

Harald Ramond expressed shock at the news of Lupe Velez's death. He claimed that he had been unable to marry her immediately because of conflicting business engagements. He denied ever asking her to sign an agreement, calling the idea "foolish." Later, he admitted that he asked her to sign the agreement: "But I didn't mean that. We had just had a fight and I was in a terrible temper."

Ramond claimed it was all a big misunderstanding. His English was not good and he thought the baby was a joke. "She pushed me out the door. I could hear the laughing on the other side."

"Who could not help love Lupe? I was proud she would consider to marry me. I am so confused. I never expected this to happen. The last time I talked to Lupe I told her I was going to marry her any way she wanted. She said she wasn't going to have a baby. So we parted."

Despite his denials, Harald Ramond could not escape his image of being a heel. At the time of Lupe's death, he was the leading choice for the coveted role of Rudolph Valentino in a screen biography. Following the scandal of Lupe's death, Ramond was removed from consideration. The role was his one chance for stardom and once he lost it, he faded into obscurity.

Lupe Velez's friends expressed disbelief upon hearing the news of her suicide. She had always seemed so full of life. Adela Rogers St. Johns wrote: "Lupe was the epitome of joyous, uninhibited lust for life. Never was there a more effervescent, earthy female Latin personality. She was so colorful and explosive as the Fourth of July."

Jimmy Durante, her frequent costar, had seen a darker side of Lupe Velez. "This great little girl was a female Pagliacci. She seemed so happy, so full of life, that you didn't think she ever had a care in the world. Did you ever see her at the fights? Hitting the canvas of the ring apron and calling out to the fighters she liked. But they used to tell me at the time of *Strike Me Pink* that she used to go to the bar at Frankie and Johnny's place and sit there all alone. I never asked her what the trouble was, for around me she seemed happy. And then out in Hollywood she got blue about some fellow, and poor kid! Well, who can see into another person's soul?"

One of the most chilling observations about her death was made by the beautiful, blonde sex symbol, Carole Landis. "I know just how she felt — you fight so long, then what have you got to face? You begin to worry about being washed up. You get bitter and disillusioned. You fear the future because there's only one way to go and that's down."

In 1948, four years after Lupe's death, Carole Landis, distraught because Rex Harrison would not marry her, stuck her head in an oven and committed suicide.

Gary Cooper, the love of Lupe's life, remained strangely silent about her death. It was rumored that he had continued to see her over the years and Lupe had not ruled out that the baby might have been his.

Her suicide was the result of personal problems and not her declining career. On December 18, she had been scheduled to go to New York for a radio broadcast. Ten days later, she was to begin a lucrative, three month nationwide personal appearance tour.

The coroner, Frank Navie, was not satisfied with the police report and demanded a full investigation of Lupe Velez's death. The district attorney, Fred Howser, uncovered no evidence of foul play. However, Beverly Hills chief of police C. H. Anderson launched an investigation into the smuggling of Seconal into the United States from Mexico. The phials of Seconal found near Lupe's bedside were from Mexico.

More than four-thousand people filed by Lupe Velez's open casket at the Church of the Recessional at Forest Lawn in Glendale. Lupe's body was flown to Mexico City for final interment. Her funeral was comparable to Rudolph Valentino's. The police were unable to control the crowd which numbered in the thousands. Lupe Velez was laid to rest in the Pateon Delores Cemetery. As the crowd pushed to get a better vantage point, monuments were knocked over and many people were injured in the crush. Lupe's sister, Reyna, fainted and was trampled by the crowd. The pallbearers included Johnny Weissmuller, Arturo de Cordova, and Gilbert Roland. There was a controversy about whether Lupe Velez, a suicide, would be allowed to be buried in consecrated ground. It was decided that she would be.

Lupe's business manager, Bo Roos, estimated the value of her estate at between $100,000 and $200,000. Velez's will left half of her estate to Beulah Kinder, with the remainder to be divided among her family. One of Lupe's sisters, Mrs. Joseph Anderson, contested the will, presenting a claim for $45,900. She proudly noted that she had saved the estate a considerable amount by preventing her sister from being buried in an expensive $12,000 bronze casket and not honoring Lupe's wish to be buried, dressed in her $15,000 ermine cape. She also removed a diamond ring, valued at $15,000 from Lupe's finger. When the estate was settled, Mrs. Anderson received $3,870 for her efforts.

Lupe Velez's possessions were auctioned on June 22, 1945. Her home, the Casa Felicitas, was sold for $41,750. Lupe's fabulous jewelry collection brought over $100,000, her chinchilla coat $25,000, and a sable coat slightly less. The rainbow shaped headboard to her bed was auctioned for only $45.

Lupe Velez provided her own epitaph: "If things turn out right, I'm glad. If not, it is destiny."

⊨ The Films of Lupe Velez ⊨

The Gaucho (United Artists, 1928). [Second billing] With Douglas Fairbanks, Geraine Greear, Eve Southern, Mary Pickford. Director, F. Richard Jones.

Stand and Deliver (Pathé, 1928). [Second billing] With Rod La Rocque, Warner Oland, Louis Natheaux, Donald Crisp. Director, Donald Crisp.

Lady of the Pavements (United Artists, 1929). [Top billing] With William Boyd, Jetta Goudal, Albert Conti, Henry Armetta, Franklin Pangborn. Director, D. W. Griffith.

Wolf Song (Paramount, 1929). [Second billing] With Gary Cooper, Louis Wolheim, Constantine Romanoff, Russ Columbo. Director, Victor Fleming.

Where East Is East (M-G-M, 1929). [Second billing] With Lon Chaney, Estelle Taylor, Lloyd Hughes, Louis Stern. Director, Tod Browning.

Tiger Rose (Warner Bros.-Vitaphone, 1929) [Second billing] With Monte Blue, Rin-Tin-Tin, H. B. Warner, Tully Marshall, Grant Withers. Director, George Fitzmaurice.

Hell Harbor (United Artists, 1930). [Top billing] With Jean Hersholt, John Holland, Gibson Gowland, Al St. John, Rondo Hatton. Director, Henry King.

The Storm (Universal, 1930) [Top billing] With Paul Cavanagh, William "Stage" Boyd, Alphone Ethier, Ernest Adams. Director, William Wyler.

East Is West (Universal, 1930). [Top billing] With Lew Ayres, Edward G. Robinson, Mary Forbes, Tetsu Komai, Henry Kolker, E. Alyn Warren. Director, Monta Bell.

Oriente Es Occidente (Spanish language version of *East Is West*) (Universal, 1930). [Top billing] With Barry Norton, Manuel Arbo, Daniel F. Rea, Tetsu Komai. Director, George Melford.

Resurrection (Universal, 1931). [Second billing] With John Boles, Nance O'Neil, William Keighley, Rose Tapley. Director, Edwin Carewe.

Resurrección (Spanish language version of *Resurrection*) (Universal, 1931). [Second billing] With Gilbert Roland, Amelia Sanisterra, Soledad Jimenez. Director, David Selman.

The Squaw Man (M-G-M, 1931). [Second billing] With Warner Baxter, Eleanor Boardman, Charles Bickford, Roland Young, Paul Cavanagh, Julia Faye. Director, Cecil B. De Mille.

The Cuban Love Song (M-G-M, 1931). [Second billing] With Lawrence Tibbett, Ernest Torrence, Jimmy Durante, Karen Morley, Louise Fazenda. Director, W. S. Van Dyke.

The Broken Wing (Paramount, 1932). [Top billing] With Leo Carrillo, Melvyn Douglas, George Barbier, Willard Robertson, Claire Dodd. Director, Lloyd Corrigan.

Hombre en Mi Vida (Spanish language version of *Men in Her Life*) (Columbia, 1932) [Top billing] With Ramon Pereda, Luis Alberni. Director, William Beaudine.

Kongo (M-G-M, 1932). [Second billing] With Walter Huston, Conrad Nagel, Virginia Bruce, C. Henry Gordon. Director, William Cowen.

The Half-Naked Truth (RKO, 1932) [Top billing] With Lee Tracy, Eugene Pallette, Frank Morgan, Bob McKenzie. Director, Gregory La Cava.

Hot Pepper (Fox, 1933). [Third billing] With Edmund Lowe, Victor McLaglen, El Brendel, Boothe Howard, Lilian Bond. Director, John Blystone.

Mr. Broadway (Broadway/Hollywood Productions, 1933). Playing herself along with Ed Sullivan, Jack Dempsey, Ruth Etting, Bert Lahr, Jack Benny, Mary Livingstone, Jack Haley, Joe Frisco, others. Director, Johnnie Walker.

Laughing Boy (M-G-M, 1934) [Second billing] With Ramon Novarro, William Davidson, Chief Thunderbird, Catalina Rambrilla. Director, W. S. Van Dyke.

Palooka (United Artists, 1934). [Second billing] With Jimmy Durante, Stuart Erwin, Marjorie Rambeau, Robert Armstrong, William Cagney, Thelma Todd. Director, Benjamin Stoloff.

Hollywood Party (M-G-M, 1934). [Second billing] With Jimmy Durante, Laurel and Hardy, Polly Moran, Ted Healy and the Three Stooges, Mickey Mouse. Director, Roy Rowland.

Strictly Dynamite (RKO, 1934). [Second billing] With Jimmy Durante, Norman Foster, William Gargan, Marlan Nixon, Eugene Pallette, Sterling Holloway. Director, Elliott Nugent.

The Morals of Marcus (Gaumont-British, 1935). [Top billing] With Ian Hunter, Adrienne Allen, Noel Madison, J. F. Roberts, Frank Atkinson. Director, Miles Mander.

Gypsy Melody (Associate British-Pathe, 1936). [Top billing] With Alfred Rode, Jerry Verno, Fred Duprey, Margaret Yarde, Raymond Lovell, Wyn Weaver. Director, Edmund T. Greville.

High Flyers (RKO, 1937). [Third billing] With Bert Wheeler, Robert Woolsey, Marjorie Lord, Margaret Dumont, Jack Carson, Paul Harvey, Charles Judels. Director, Edward Cline.

La Zandunga (Film Selectos, 1938). [Top billing] With Rafael Falcon, Arturo de Cordova, Joaquin Pardave, Carlos Lopez Chaflan, Maria Luisa Zea. Director, Fernando de Fuentes.

Mad About Money (British Lion, 1938). [Second billing] With Ben Lyon, Wallace Ford, Jean Collin, Harry Langdon, Mary Cole, Cyril Raymond. Director, Meville Brown.

The Girl From Mexico (RKO, 1939). [Top billing] With Donald Woods, Leon Errol, Linda Hayes, Donald MacBride, Elisabeth Risdon, Ward Bond. Director, Leslie Goodwins.

Mexican Spitfire (RKO, 1939). [Top billing] With Donald Woods, Leon Errol, Linda Hayes, Elisabeth Risdon, Cecil Kellaway, Charles Coleman. Director, Leslie Goodwins.

Mexican Spitfire Out West (RKO, 1940). [Top billing] With Donald Woods, Leon Errol, Linda Hayes, Grant Withers, Elisabeth Risdon, Cecil Kellaway. Director, Leslie Goodwins.

Recordar Es Visir (Pereda, 1941). Compilation feature with segments of Mexican sound films including Lupe Velez from *La Zandunga,* and Lupita Tovar, Tito Guizar, Cantinflas, etc.

Six Lessons From Madame La Zonga (Universal, 1941). [Top billing] With Leon Errol, Helen Parrish, Charles Lang, Guinn "Big Boy" Williams, William Frawley. Director, John Rawlins.

Mexican Spitfire's Baby (RKO, 1941). [Top billing] With Leon Errol, Charles "Buddy" Rogers, ZaSu Pitts, Elisabeth Risdon, Marion Martin, Lloyd Corrigan. Director, Leslie Goodwins.

Playmates (RKO, 1941). [Third billing] With Kay Kyser, John Barrymore, Ginny Simms, May Robson, Patsy Kelly, Peter Lind Hayes, Harry Babbitt, Ish Kabibble. Director, David Butler.

Honolulu Lu (Columbia, 1941). [Top billing] With Bruce Bennett, Leo Carrillo, Marjorie Gateson, Forrest Tucker, Lloyd Bridges, Don Beddoe. Director, Charles Barton.

Mexican Spitfire at Sea (RKO, 1942) [Top billing] With Leon Errol, Charles "Buddy" Rogers, ZaSu Pitts, Elisabeth Risdon, Marion Martin, Florence Bates. Director, Leslie Goodwins.

Mexican Spitfire Sees a Ghost (RKO, 1942). [Top billing] With Leon Errol, Charles "Buddy" Rogers, Elisabeth Risdon, Donald MacBride, Minna Gombell. Director, Leslie Goodwins.

Mexican Spitfire's Elephant (RKO, 1942). [Top billing] With Leon Errol, Walter Reed, Lyle Talbot, Elisabeth Risdon, Marion Martin, Luis Alberni. Director, Leslie Goodwins.

Ladies' Day (RKO, 1943). [Top billing] With Eddie Albert, Patsy Kelly, Max Baer, Jerome Cowan, Iris Adrian, Cliff Clark, Joan Barclay. Director, Leslie Goodwins.

Mexican Spitfire's Blessed Event (RKO, 1943). [Top billing] With Leon Errol, Walter Reed, Hugh Beaumont, Elisabeth Risdon, Wally Brown, Alan Carney. Director, Leslie Goodwins.

Redhead From Manhattan (Columbia, 1943). [Top billing] With Michael Duane, Tim Ryan, Gerald Mohr, Lilian Yarbo, Arthur Loft, Lewis Wilson. Director, Lew Landers.

Nana (Santander Producers, 1944). [Top billing] With Miguel Angel Ferriz, Chela Castro, Crox Alvarado, Elena D'Orgaz, Sergio Orta. Director, Clestino Gorostiza.

Bibliography

Books

Anger, Kenneth. *Hollywood Babylon.* Dell, 1981.
_____. *Hollywood Babylon* II. Plume, 1985.
Arce, Hector. *Gary Cooper.* Morrow, 1979.
Autry, Gene. *Back in the Saddle Again.* Doubleday, 1978.
Bergreen, Laurence. *As Thousands Cheer.* Viking, 1990.
Bosworth, Patricia. *Montgomery Clift.* Bantam, 1978.
Bradshaw, Jon. *Dreams That Money Can Buy.* Morrow, 1985.
Brian, Dennis. *Tallulah Darling.* Macmillan, 1972.
Brownlow, Kevin. *The Parade's Gone By.* Ballantine, 1968.
Cagney, James and Warren, Doug. *Cagney.* St. Martin's, 1983.
Carey, Gary, *All the Stars in Heaven.* Dutton, 1981.
_____. *Doug & Mary.* Dutton, 1977.
Carpozi, George. *The Gary Cooper Story.* Arlington House, 1970.

Carter, Randolph. *The World of Flo Ziegfeld*. Praeger, 1974.

Davies, Marion. *The Times We Had*. Bobbs-Merrill, 1975.

De Mille, Cecil B. *The Autobiography of Cecil B. De Mille*. Prentice Hall, 1959.

Dempsey, Jack. *Dempsey*. Harper & Row, 1977.

Dickens, Homer. *The Films of Gary Cooper*. Citadel, 1970.

Duarte, John. *The Heavyweight Champions*. Hastings House, 1964.

Eels, George. *Ginger, Loretta, and Irene Who?* Putnam, 1976.

_____. *The Life That Late He Led*. Putnam, 1967.

Everson, William. *The Films of Laurel & Hardy*. Citadel, 1967.

Eyman, Scott. *Mary Pickford*. Donald Fine Inc., 1990.

Fairbanks, Jr., Douglas. *The Salad Days*. Doubleday, 1988.

Feinman, Jeffrey. *Hollywood Confidential*. Playboy, 1976.

Finch, Christopher and Rosenkrantz, Linda. *Gone Hollywood*. Doubleday, 1979.

Fountain Gilbert, Leatrice. *Dark Star*. St. Martin's, 1985.

Flynn, Errol. *My Wicked, Wicked Ways*. Putnam, 1959.

Forrester, Tom. *The Stooges' Lost Episode*. Contemporary, 1988.

Fowler, Gene. *Schnozolla*. Viking, 1951.

Fradella, Sal. *Jack Johnson*. Branden, 1989.

Goldman, Herbert. *Fannie Brice*. Oxford, 1992.

Grossman, Barbara. *Funny Woman*. Indiana University Press, 1991.

Harris, Warren G. *Cary Grant.* Zebra, 1987.

_____. *Gable & Lombard.* Simon & Schuster, 1974.

Head, Edith and Calistro, Paddy (Autobiography of Edith Head). Dutton, 1983.

Heymann, C. David. *Poor Little Rich Girl.* Lyle Stuart, 1983.

Higham, Charles. *Cary Grant.* Harcourt, Brace, Jovanovich, 1969.

_____. *Cecil B. De Mille.* Charles Scribner's Sons, 1973.

_____. *Marlene.* W. W. Norton, 1977.

_____. *Orson Welles.* St. Martin's, 1985.

Jacobson, Laurie. *Hollywood Heartbreak.* Fireside, 1984.

Jennings, Dean. *We Only Kill Each Other.* Prentice Hall, 1967.

Kael, Pauline, *The Citizen Kane Book.* Atlantic Monthly, 1971.

Kaminsky, Stuart. *Coop.* St. Martin's, 1980.

Katkov, Norman. *The Fabulous Fanny.* Alfred A. Knopf, 1953.

Kobal, John. *People Will Talk.* Alfred A. Knopf, 1985.

Kobler, John. *Damned in Paradise.* Atheneum, 1977.

Koury, Phil. *Yes, Mr. De Mille.* Putnam, 1959.

La Guardia, Robert. *Monty.* Arbor House, 1977.

Lahr, John. *Notes on a Cowardly Lion.* Alfred A. Knopf, 1969.

Lambert, Gavin. *Norma Shearer.* Alfred A. Knopf, 1990.

Levin, Martin. *Hollywood and the Great Fan Magazines.* Castle, 1970.

Lloyd, Ann and Fuller, Graham. *The Illustrated Who's Who of the Cinema*. Macmillan, 1983.

Lloyd, Ann. *Movies of the Silent Years*. Orbis, 1984.

Loy, Myrna and Kotsilibas-Davis, James. *Myrna Loy*. Alfred A. Knopf, 1987.

Machlin, Milt. *Libby*. Tower, 1980.

Marx, Arthur. *Red Skelton*. Dutton, 1979.

Maxwell, Elsa. *RSVP*. Little Brown, 1954.

Mc Cabe, John. *Charlie Chaplin*. Doubleday, 1978.

_____. *Laurel & Hardy*. Ballentine, 1975.

Medved, Harry and Medved, Michael. *The Golden Turkey Awards*. Berkley, 1980.

Miller, Don, *B Movies*. Ballantine, 1988.

Mix, Paul. *The Life and Legend of Tom Mix*. A. S. Barnes, 1972.

Moore, Colleen. *Silent Star*. Doubleday, 1968.

Nash, Jay Robert. *Bloodletters and Badmen*. M. Evans & Co., 1973.

_____. *Zanies*. New Century, 1982.

Nicholas, John. *Tom Mix*. Persimmon Hill, 1980.

Oakie, Jack. *Double Takes*. Strawberry Hill, 1980.

Parish, James Robert. *The Hollywood Death Book*. Pioneer, 1992.

_____. *The RKO Gals*. Arlington House, 1974.

_____ and Marill, Alvin H. *The Cinema of Edward G. Robinson*. A. S. Barnes, 1972.

Parsons, Louella. *The Gay Illiterate*. Garden City, 1945.

Peters, Margot. *The House of Barrymore*. Alfred A. Knopf, 1990.

Reynolds, Patrick and Shachtman, Tom. *The Gilded Leaf*. Little Brown, 1989.

Ringgold, Gene and Bodeen, DeWitt. *The Films of Cecil B. De Mill.* Citadel, 1969.

Roberts, Randy. *Jack Dempsey.* LSU Press, 1979.

Robinson, David. *Charlie Chaplin.* McGraw-Hill, 1985.

Robinson, Edward G. *All My Yesterdays.* Hawthorn, 1973.

Schelly, William. *Harry Langdon.* Scarecrow, 1982.

Schulberg, Budd. *Moving Pictures.* Stein and Day, 1981.

Siegel, Scott and Siegel, Barbara. *The Encyclopedia of Hollywood.* Facts on File, 1990.

Silverman, Stephen. *The Fox That Got Away.* Lyle Stuart, 1988.

Skretvedt, Randy. *Laurel and Hardy.* Moonstone, 1987.

Springer, John and Hamilton, Jack. *They Had Faces Then.* Castle, 1974.

Stenn, David. *Clara Bow.* Doubleday, 1988.

St. Johns, Adela Rogers. *Love, Laughter, and Tears.* Doubleday, 1978.

Swindell, Larry. *The Last Hero.* Doubleday, 1980.

_____. *Screwball.* Morrow, 1975.

Thomas, Bob. *Thalberg.* Doubleday, 1967.

Thomas, Tony and Terry, Jim. *The Busby Berkeley Book,* New York Graphic Society, 1973.

Tibbets, John and Welsh, James. *His Majesty the American.* A. S. Barnes, 1977.

Tuska, Jon. *The Filming of the West.* Doubleday, 1976.

Wallace, Amy; Wallenchinsky, David; and Wallace, Irving. *Book of Lists 3.* Morrow, 1983.

Wallace, Irving; Wallace, Amy; Wallechinsky, David; and Wallace, Sylvia. *The Intimate Lives of Famous People*. Delacorte, 1981.

Wallechinsky, David. *The Complete Book of the Olympics*. Penguin, 1988.

Wayne, Jane Ellen. *Cooper's Women*. Prentice Hall, 1988.

Wiaschin, Ken. *The World's Great Movie Stars*. Harmony, 1979.

Wilk, Max. *Every Day's a Matinee*. W. W. Norton, 1975.

Wilkerson, Tichi and Borie, Marcia. *The Hollywood Reporters*. Coward McCann, 1984.

Windeler, Robert. *Sweetheart*. Praeger, 1974.